SPOOKY

Georgia

Also in the Spooky Series by
S. E. Schlosser and Paul G. Hoffman:

Spooky California
Spooky Campfire Tales
Spooky Canada
Spooky Colorado
Spooky Florida
Spooky Indiana
Spooky Maryland
Spooky Massachusetts
Spooky Michigan
Spooky Montana
Spooky New England
Spooky New Jersey
Spooky New York
Spooky North Carolina
Spooky Oregon
Spooky Pennsylvania
Spooky South
Spooky South Carolina
Spooky Southwest
Spooky Texas
Spooky Virginia
Spooky Washington
Spooky Wisconsin

SPOOKY
Georgia

*Tales of Hauntings, Strange Happenings,
and Other Local Lore*

RETOLD BY S. E. SCHLOSSER

ILLUSTRATED BY PAUL G. HOFFMAN

Guilford, Connecticut

Project editor: Meredith Dias

Text design/layout: Lisa Reneson, Two Sisters Design
Map by Alena Pearce © Rowman & Littlefield

Library of Congress Cataloging-in-Publication Data is available on file.

ISBN 978-0-7627-6420-4

Printed in the United States of America

Distributed by NATIONAL BOOK NETWORK

For my family: David, Dena, Tim, Arlene,
Hannah, Emma, Nathan, Ben, Deb, Gabe,
Clare, Jack, Chris, Karen, Davey, and Aunt Mil

For Erin Turner, Paul Hoffman,
and all the wonderful folks at Globe Pequot Press,
with my thanks

Contents

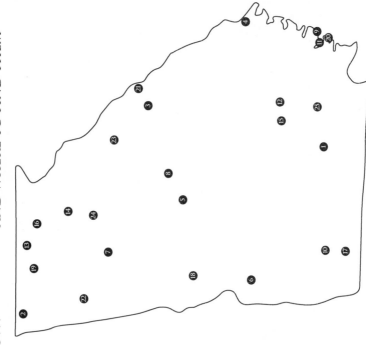

Contents

Introduction

I walked along the marsh path in the predawn light, my SLR camera heavy around my neck and the smell of the sea washing over me. It was a warm January morning and I was up betimes, hoping to locate one of the "Island Treasures" hidden each day by Jekyll Island Authority volunteers. The island treasure hunt took place throughout the month of January, and the hidden "treasures" were collectable glass floats, replicas of the floats used by fishermen in the early 1900s. I'd read about the floats in the island newspaper over dinner last night and was eager to put my detecting skills to work.

As I neared the beach, I saw a distorted figure looming against the dawn. My pulse gave a little jump of fear, and then I realized I was looking at a dead tree, worn to smoothness by wind and waves. I must have stumbled inadvertently upon the famous Driftwood Beach! I'd heard it was on the north end of the island, but who knew it was right next door to my condo?

Glass floats forgotten, I hauled up my SLR and started shooting photos of the driftwood silhouetted against the rising sun. A fishing boat riding through the sun-licked waves amid a cloud of seagulls completed the lovely picture. I sighed in sheer delight and took a seat on a fallen giant, leaning my head against the silvery wood.

When the sun was well and truly up and gulls and grackles had taken possession of the beach, I tore myself away and headed back to the condo. If found my sister and five-year-old nephew awake and raring to go, so I hustled them into the car and drove north to St. Simon's Island, our spooky destination for the day. We were booked on a historical tour and then planned to climb the lighthouse, which we had seen when we wandered the north beach earlier this week. What we hadn't planned was a close encounter with the dead lighthouse keeper ("The Lighthouse"). I really shouldn't have been surprised. After all, the three of us descended from a Pennsylvania Dutch Powwow Doctor. Supernatural encounters are to be expected.

My tour of spooky Georgia began in Atlanta, where a musical ghost once stalked a murderer ("Bell Ringer") and Civil War physicians still haunt the suburbs ("The Operation"). The ghost of a Civil War soldier helped bring his killer to justice in the town of Cuthbert, and a Revolutionary Patriot led a homeless old lady to his buried treasure in Chatsworth.

Ghosts aren't the only supernatural residents in Georgia. A werewolf once plagued Talbot County ("Isabella"), and a railroad engineer encountered Bigfoot in Lawrenceville ("On the Tracks"). Then there was the nineteenth-century doctor who saw a UFO on his way home from a difficult birth ("Silver"), not to mention Abram's close encounter with the devil ("The Devil Is Going to Get You").

The culmination of my *Spooky Georgia* research trip came on my last night in Savannah, when a very active ghost paid a dramatic visit to my hotel suite ("Shave and a Haircut"). Scared the dickens out of my sister and me. My nephew slept through the whole thing!

Georgia is a mysterious and lovely state. When I close my eyes, I can still see the sun rising over Driftwood Beach and feel the warm breeze caressing my hair. And I can still hear the voices of my friends, young and old, eager and frightened, relating the supernatural stories that are as much a part of their Georgia heritage as the land and sea.

I hope you enjoy their stories as much as I do.

—Sandy Schlosser

PART ONE
Ghost Stories

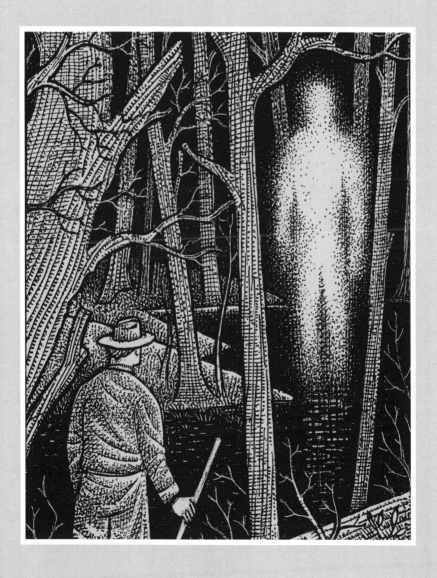

1

$\mathscr{B}urnt\ \mathscr{C}hurch$

LAKELAND

She was sophisticated, poised, and cultured. In retrospect, this should have made them suspicious. A teacher like her should be presiding over a girl's school in London or New York, not seeking a position in a small town in Georgia. But at the time they were too delighted by her application to ask any questions.

"It will be good for our daughter to learn some culture," the attorney's wife told the pastor's wife.

"And our boy may find some table manners at last," the pastor's wife responded with a smile.

School was called into session in the local church shortly after the arrival of the teacher. And soon the children were bringing glowing reports home. "Teacher" was special. Teacher taught them manners and diction as well as reading, writing, and arithmetic. All the children loved Teacher.

The parents were delighted by the progress their children were making at school. Teacher had been a real find. A godsend, said the preacher's wife.

But not everyone in town was so satisfied. The local ne'er-do-well, called Smith, had more sinister stories to tell.

"That woman ain't natural," he told the blacksmith, waving a bottle of whisky for emphasis. "I seen her out in the woods after dark, dancing around a campfire and chanting in a strange language."

"Nonsense," the blacksmith retorted, calmly hammering a headed iron bar on his anvil.

"They say she's got an altar in her room, and it ain't an altar to the Almighty," Smith insisted, leaning forward and blowing his boozy breath into the blacksmith's face.

"You're drunk," said the blacksmith, lifting the hot iron to bar the man from coming any closer. "Go home and sleep it off."

Smith left the smithy, but he continued to talk wild about the teacher in the weeks that followed. During those weeks a change gradually came over the schoolchildren. The typical high jinks and pranks that all children played lessened. Their laughter died away. And when they did misbehave, it was on a much more ominous scale than before. Items began to disappear from houses and farms—valuable items like jewelry, farm tools, and money. When children talked back to their parents, there was a hard edge to their voices, and they did not apologize for their rudeness, even when punished.

"And my daughter lied to me the other day," the attorney's wife said to the pastor's wife in distress. "I saw her punch her younger brother and steal an apple from him, and she denied it to my face. She practically called me a liar!"

"The games the children play back in the woods frighten me," the pastor's wife confessed. "They chant in a strange language, and they move in such a strange manner. Almost like a ritual dance."

"Could it be something they are learning at school?" asked the attorney's wife.

BURNT CHURCH

"Surely not! Teacher is such a sweet, sophisticated lady," said the pastor's wife.

But they exchanged uneasy glances.

Smith, on the other hand, was sure. "That teacher is turning the young'uns to the devil, that's what she's doing," he proclaimed up and down the streets of the town.

"Don't be ridiculous," the preacher told him when they passed in front of the mercantile.

"I ain't ridiculous. You are blind," Smith told him. "That teacher ought to be burned at the stake."

The pastor, pale with wrath, ordered Smith out of his sight. But the ne'er-do-well's words rang in his mind and would not be pushed away. And the children continued to behave oddly. Almost like they were possessed. He would, the preacher decided reluctantly, have to look into it someday soon.

That day came sooner than he thought. The very next Monday his little boy came down with a cold, and his mother kept him home from school. When the pastor returned from his duties for a late lunch, his wife came running up to him as soon as he entered the door. She was pale with fright.

"I heard him chanting something over and over again in his bedroom," she gasped. "So I crept to the door to listen. He was saying the Lord's Prayer backwards!"

The pastor gasped and clutched his Bible to his chest, as goose bumps erupted over his body. This was positively satanic. And there was nowhere the boy could have learned such a thing in this town, unless he learned it . . . at school.

At that moment the attorney's wife came bursting in the door behind him.

"Quick, Pastor, quick," she cried. "Smith is running through town with a torch, talking about burning down the school. The children are still in class!"

The pastor raced out of the house with the two women at his heels. They and the other townsfolk who followed them were met by a huge cloud of smoke coming from the direction of the church, where the schoolchildren had their lessons. The building was already ablaze as frantic parents beat at the flames with wet sacks or threw buckets of water from the pump into the inferno. Smith could be heard cackling unrepentantly from the far side of the building, which was full of the screams of the trapped students and their teacher.

The fire blazed with a supernatural kind of force, and the pastor thought he heard the sound of the teacher laughing from within the building when it became apparent that no one could be saved.

The church burned for several hours, and when the flames were finally extinguished, there was virtually nothing left. Mourning parents tried to find something of their children to bury, and Smith wisely disappeared from town, his mission against the works of Satan completed.

The teacher's burnt body was buried deep in the ground and covered with a brick tomb. The children's smaller bodies were interred beneath wooden crosses. Of all the students in the school that fall, only the pastor's small son survived.

To this day voices can be heard in the graveyard of Burnt Church, chanting unintelligible words, as the school children and the teacher once chanted in the woods outside town. Sometimes apparitions are seen, and dark walkers roam the graveyard at night. And they say that a brick taken from the grave of the evil teacher can set fire to objects on which it is placed.

6

2

Lightning Brigade

CHICKAMAUGA BATTLEFIELD

I don't do ghosts. Never believed in any of that rot. Which makes the story I am going to relate very difficult to explain.

I was staying with friends in Fort Oglethorpe for a week. Tim was a buddy of mine who'd been in the same platoon in Iraq. We'd mustered out about the same time but kept in touch. He invited me down to his place to celebrate Thanksgiving with the family, and naturally I was interested in visiting Chickamauga Battlefield, having studied it when I was in the military.

I was out of bed before dawn and out for a jog not much later. Tim suggested taking a route through the battlefield park, and I couldn't think of a better way to see Chickamauga.

It was one of those misty mornings you sometimes get before a gorgeous day. I could tell there was bright sunshine coming behind the fog, but when I started out, it was hard to see anything but billows of white mist. I didn't see many cars about so early, and when I turned onto Lafayette Road, I was the only one there.

My skin prickled as I entered the park. I thought it must be excitement. I'd always wanted to visit Chickamauga Battlefield— scene of the second-bloodiest battle in the Civil War. The battle was lost by the Union because of misinformation and a coincidence—something that could happen to anyone.

The mist was still thick as I jogged past the visitor center with its big guns out front, remembering all I'd learned about the battle. A second shiver ran through me at the sight of the canons. I could almost hear the huge boom of those guns, and the mist around me could have been smoke.

Following the tour signs, I swung a left onto Alexander's Bridge Road and then took a right on Battleline Road. Monuments rose out of the mist, honoring the fallen and the valiant battalions that fought on both sides. The mist was thicker under the trees, and the solemn stone eyes of the soldiers carved in stone made the back of my neck itch. I was jogging the battle line, and I could almost sense the two forces massed against each other on either side of me.

The battle started late because the Confederate General Bragg's orders went astray. The Confederates attacked the northern flank of the Union Army in midmorning, and things didn't look so good for the Southern forces. Then, in one of those unforgettable moments in military history, Union Brigadier General Rosecrans received a missive claiming that a gap had formed in the Union line. Not taking time to verify the report, Rosecrans scrambled to fill it...

I rounded a bend and saw the Georgia monument looming out of the mist. There was an open field here, and the mist was burning off rapidly. The air seemed lighter somehow as I came to the intersection with Lafayette Road. I turned right and almost immediately saw the replica of the Brotherton cabin. I felt another shiver run right down my spine. The Brotherton cabin—and the gap. . . .

In an attempt to fill the mythical gap in the Union line, Rosecrans created a real one—with disastrous consequences. In one of those crazy coincidences that litter history, right at the moment that the Union general pulled his men out of the line to fill a nonexistent gap, Confederate troops came sweeping out of the woods and rushed to attack the Union line. I could almost see them rising from the mist and barreling past me as I jogged past the Brotherton cabin. The Confederates were probably mystified when the expected enemy firing did not commence, and they rushed unhindered through the gap. I shuddered at such a tactical error on the part of the Union forces. The Confederate attack broke the Union divisions, creating complete chaos.

A short way down the road, I veered for a moment into Viniard's Field as the mist around me lightened with the rising sun. This was the scene of the bloodiest action in the battle. Fighting went back and forth across Lafayette Road, and the record claimed that a person could walk across the field on the bodies of the slain without setting foot on the ground. I swallowed hard. I'd lost a few comrades in Iraq, and something about this mist-shrouded field with its canon and monuments to the fallen brought it all back. I turned abruptly and headed back to the road, my mind alive with memories.

The fog was white and patchy as I swung a right onto Glenn-Viniard Road. I was now heading toward a short tower at the top of a small hill—the monument honoring the Wilder Brigade. Trees closed around me again for a moment, and the mist thickened as I drove away painful thoughts of my personal past with historical remembrances about this part of the battlefield.

The only Union troops left intact when the Confederates swarmed through the gap were members of the Lightning Brigade under Col. John T. Wilder. The Lightning Brigade—so named because they rode their horses as swiftly as they could into the battlefield and then dismounted to fight as infantrymen— were armed with brand-new seven-shot Spencer repeating rifles, purchased with their own money. The brigade occupied a hill at the southern end of the battlefield and kept the Confederates at bay long enough to cover the chaotic retreat of the routed Union soldiers.

On impulse, I turned into the parking area below the tower on the hill and jogged through the lot to a path that led to the monument at the summit. The mist had gone white again and thinned under the heat of the early-morning sun as I jogged out of the parking lot onto the path.

And found myself in the middle of a huge cloud of smoke, gunpowder stinging my eyes as a thunderclap of canon fire deafened me. I gasped, coughing and sputtering, and stopped in my tracks. What in the name of all that was holy?

As the smoke cleared I saw a boy in Union blue loading a Spencer rifle with seven shots. He aimed at something behind me and fired repeatedly. I heard gunfire behind me, and I hit the ground, bullets whizzing all around me. My eyes stayed on the boy. Surely he wasn't old enough to be a soldier, I thought, dazed. I became aware of men in blue all around us, shooting and reloading. I rolled over, sat up, and stared across a sea of gray down below, surging determinedly toward this summit. Bodies were strewn everywhere. Almost beside me lay a gray-clad figure with half his face blown away. One of his eyeballs hung by a thread. My stomach roiled at the sight.

LIGHTNING BRIGADE

I lurched to my feet and pushed my way through the rapidly firing soldiers. None of them saw me. My foot kicked a half-filled canteen fallen from the hand of a dead soldier. It bounced away. The canon fired again, sending smoke everywhere. Instinctively I headed for the summit of the hill and found myself looking up at a soldier on horseback. His was a face out of the history books—Col. John T. Wilder, looking grim, haggard, and too thin. The troops didn't have enough food, I recalled. Our eyes met.

Then a beam of sunlight shot down from overhead, piercing the smoke from the canon fire, which was not smoke at all but mist. And the sounds of battle were replaced by the early-morning twitter of birds.

My shoulder was aching from where I'd hit the ground, and I had plant debris and dirt clinging to my jogging pants. I stared around me, shocked by the return of normalcy after such an encounter. My heart pounded madly, and every nerve in my body twanged. What just happened? Without conscious thought, I found myself fleeing the hilltop at speed, my mind a roaring white blankness. Around me, the mist burned away as full daylight brought the world awake. I loped past a herd of deer in Dyer Field, barely registering their presence, and didn't take the planned loop up to Snodgrass Hill where General Thomas, the "Rock of Chickamauga," held off Confederate attacks all day while Union forces retreated back to Chattanooga.

I was vaguely surprised at how fast I was going, considering how far I'd already jogged that morning. But adrenaline can do that to a person. I only slowed when my legs started shaking with fatigue. I dropped to a walk as I reached the end of the loop and turned onto Lafayette Road again. It was considerably busier now. Blessedly so. I needed a strong dose of reality after those shocking moments on the hill. I picked up a jog again, wondering if I should tell my buddy about the ghostly encounter. Nah, I decided as I entered the driveway. Why bother? Tim didn't believe in ghosts.

3

The Headache

RICHMOND COUNTY

It was one the slaves who found my grown son lying dead on his bed and his former nurse, Lila, who came into my dressing room to tell me the news. Lila was wringing her hands and weeping, so I knew something was wrong. My son, Paul, who oversaw the running of the plantation, had not appeared at the usual time to give out the daily work assignments. The man sent to check on him found him lying lifeless in his chamber.

I gasped, pulled on a robe, and rushed to see for myself. Paul lay unmoving on the bed. I could tell at once he wasn't breathing, and when I touched his body, it was cold. I sent one of the servants for the doctor, though I knew he could not help us. Then I sat numbly in the chair beside the bed, staring at my son's handsome face, so still in death, and thinking about all the sacrifices he had made for his family over the years.

My husband died while Paul was still attending university, and I had no one to tend the plantation except for my husband's overseer, whom I did not like. Rand Folsom bullied the slaves and was surly with me. My husband could manage him—just— but he ignored my orders whenever he thought he could get away with it. So my son left his dearly loved university to take over the running of the plantation.

It was the perfect solution, and my son made the sacrifice gladly. The slaves loved Paul. They had watched him grow up, ride his first horse, tell his first joke. When Paul, on his first day home, reprimanded the overseer for his cruel methods right in front of the slaves, their loyalty was assured.

My son and Rand Folsom argued daily. Paul and I had discussed dismissing the overseer over dinner a few nights before his death. It would be a hassle, training a new overseer to our ways, but in the long run it would work out much better for all of us. But now . . .

I reached over and took my son's cold hand in mine. I couldn't think about the future right now. It was too much for me to cope with.

The doctor could not account for Paul's sudden death. Paul must have had a heart attack or a stroke, he told me sadly, shaking his head. He found it strange that Paul had shown no symptoms of either before dying so precipitously.

The arrival of the doctor triggered the tears that I had held in abeyance all morning. I collapsed into my daughter's arms and was taken to my room to lie down while the servants and the doctor did what they must for my poor dead son.

But the work must go on. While I lay in my room, ill from grief, Rand Folsom took over the work of the plantation. I came down briefly for the funeral and then retreated again to my misery. Even in my aerie, I heard that the overseer had resumed his cruel bullying. The slaves were miserable once more, as they often had been before Paul came home from university. I would have to do something about the situation—as soon as my strength returned, I decided.

THE HEADACHE

The thought brought me out of my grief enough to rise the next morning and make my way downstairs. I had barely sat down to breakfast when Lily, Paul's old nurse, came to see me.

"Miz McKellam, something is wrong," she said, wringing her hands. "I don't like to trouble you, but you got to know about this. I was praying in the church yesterday, kneeling before the altar, and I saw Mr. Paul sitting on the steps before me, holding his head in his hands like he had a terrible headache. Something is wrong 'bout his death, and he won't rest in peace until it is righted."

I went pale and swayed in my chair. She'd seen Paul's ghost? That seemed impossible. I shook my head to clear it and said, "I understand you are upset about Mr. Paul's death, Lily, but I don't want you to spread stories like that." Our eyes met for a heartbeat, and I knew she was telling me the truth. I didn't know what to do about it.

"Yes Ma'am," she said.

I thought the matter had been dropped, but that evening Big Jim, my son's personal servant, came to see me.

"Miz McKellam, I saw Paul today," Big Jim said without preamble. "He was pacing back and forth under the big water oak and holding his head in his hands like it hurt him something terrible. He looked straight at me, and his face was crumpled in pain."

I grabbed the back of a chair before my knees buckled. Twice in one day! It seemed impossible. I looked into Big Jim's eyes and saw pain there that echoed my own. He truly believed what he was telling me. But could I trust the servants in this matter? Perhaps, in their sorrow, they were seeing things. I thanked Big Jim for telling me about the ghost and let the matter drop.

Several days passed while my strength gradually returned. The reports coming to me about Rand Folsom were troubling. I was going to have to dismiss the man as soon as I was steady on my feet.

Early one afternoon a neighbor from the nearby plantation paid me a call. I decided to ask her for a recommendation for a new overseer during the course of our visit. But the thought went right out of my head when, over tea and biscuits, she told me she had been sent by her slaves to give me a message. Her people, whose word she trusted, had seen Paul wandering through the fields, clutching his head as if he was in pain. I gasped and my eyes met those of my friend. She was sincere. Her people had seen my son's ghost, just as his beloved nurse and personal servant had.

This was the third time my son had attempted to communicate with us. I had to do something. My friend and I discussed the matter and agreed that Paul's body must be exhumed. I sent a message to the doctor, who came to the plantation to examine my son's body again, focusing this time on the young man's head.

After a careful examination, the doctor found a nail that had been driven into Paul's head by some unknown person. My son had been murdered. The small wound had been hidden by his hair when the doctor examined him the first time.

There was only one person on the plantation with access to the nails, which were locked in the carpenter shop. That person was Rand Folsom, the overseer my son had intended to discharge from his long-held position.

The overseer was arrested following the discovery of the murder. As soon as he heard the slaves' testimony regarding my son's ghost, Folsom confessed. He was hung on August 11, 1831.

Paul's ghost was never seen again.

4

Shave and a Haircut

SAVANNAH

I wasn't thinking about ghosts when I checked into my Savannah hotel. Too busy running after my five-year-old nephew and chatting to his mother—my younger sister—to pay heed to the supernatural stories circulating about our hotel. And my sixth sense certainly didn't pick up anything particularly alarming when I entered our suite.

There were two bedrooms in the suite. A loft bedroom overlooked the two-story living room, with a rather grand carpeted staircase rising up to it. The rest of the suite contained the hallway, kitchen, bathroom, and back bedroom. I smiled and went to claim the back bedroom, allowing my sister the larger upstairs bedroom, which had a TV as well as a big bed and space for my nephew's toys

While my sister and my nephew were settling themselves in, I unpacked. Then I moved through the entire downstairs suite, clearing the space and putting up various supernatural protections as I always did when traveling. Better safe than sorry.

My sister and her little red-haired boy came down from their bedroom and joined me in the living room to discuss the agenda for our stay. With only a weekend to spend in Savannah and surrounds, I needed to make good use of every moment to do folklore research for my book. While I reviewed options, my sister read the room journal where previous guests shared comments and experiences. My sister looked up with a grin and said, "This one is for you, folklorist! There's a ghost in this hotel." She began reading excerpts and showing me various pages of the journal; fascinating stuff but not exactly conducive to weekend planning.

We went down to the front desk to book a ghost tour, and in the process we learned the story of the ghost from one of the hotel staff. The original building had caught fire sometime in the late 1800s. Although the fire company was quick to respond, the entire building was soon ablaze, and the day ended in a total loss. The origins of the fire were never established, but legend suggested that the hotel ghost—who was very friendly, the staff member emphasized, looking at my little nephew—was someone who had died in the flames.

After dinner the three of us took a trolley ghost tour around the city. My nephew listened pop-eyed and silent to the costumed narrator, but he wasn't too spooked as long as Mommy was with him.

My sixth sense twitched as soon as we stopped at the Colonial Cemetery. While the narrator told spooky stories, I took several photos of the various tombstones visible from over the iron fence. Sure enough, when I checked my camera, I had a white mist near one of the graves I'd photographed. A moment later, the tour guide swung her hand in that general direction and talked about the spirits haunting that particular section of the cemetery. I decided not to mention what I'd seen in my photo.

The rest of the ghost tour was interesting, from a folklore perspective, but uneventful supernaturally, which was fine by me. The last week of my trip had been a bit too full of ghostly activity for my peace of mind. The paternal side of my family had always been sensitive to the supernatural, descending as we did from a Pennsylvania Dutch powwow doctor, and paranormal activity seemed to multiply with three of us visiting haunted locations.

We put ourselves and the kidling to bed after the tour, which had kept my nephew up far past his scheduled bedtime. I slept like a log, but my sister was a bit blurry eyed the next morning. She was creeped out by the full-length mirror hanging at the top of the grand staircase opposite the bed. I told her I'd cover it for her that night so she could sleep better, and then I forgot all about it in the rush to get to our day's activities.

After a morning tour of Savannah we had lunch at the haunted Pirate House restaurant (which really is haunted, both my sister and I confirmed). An invisible fourth person attached himself to us shortly after we reached our table in the Herb House section of the restaurant, and my sister told me it was a little boy before the waitstaff even mentioned the little boy ghost that haunted the house. He seemed particularly taken with my nephew. Needless to say, I got some more spooky pictures during that memorable lunch!

In the afternoon my sister and her son took a nap at the hotel while I went to three more haunted locations: The lighthouse on Tybee Island, spooky Fort Scriven (that place gave me the heebie-jeebies), and Fort Pulaski. Our family regrouped at 5:30, and we spent the evening at the River Walk and then watched a little TV before retiring for the night. Following the show I helped my sister cover the upsetting mirror at the top of the stairs and then headed downstairs to my bedroom to take some notes on what I'd seen and heard during the day. Then I turned off the light and dropped immediately into a deep sleep.

I was abruptly awakened around midnight when my door slammed open and my sister rushed in with my nephew and his blankets in her arms. "I need your help," she said. "He won't stop knocking. You need to go up there and make him stop. I can't sleep." She put my sleeping nephew on my vacated spot on the bed.

After triple-checking that her somnolent son was okay, my sister dragged me out the door. "He won't stop," she reiterated, just in case I'd missed her message the first time. "You need to talk to the ghost and make him stop the knocking."

My adrenaline had kicked in with my sister's abrupt arrival, and I followed her down the hallway, ready for anything. As soon as I turned the corner into the living room and the bottom of the staircase, I heard a hollow banging. *Rap-rap. Rap-rap-rap-rap.* Someone or something was knocking on the wall beside the covered mirror at the top of the stairs.

"It's probably just the people in the next suite," I reassured my trembling sister. Not that either of us believed it. My sixth sense had told me there was a ghost as soon as I left my bedroom. But I didn't want to freak her out more than she already was.

The light beside the bed was on. I could see the staircase and the shrouded mirror quite clearly as I climbed the stairs, though other parts of the balcony bedroom were shadowed, since my sister had closed the shades on the skylights. As I reached the top of the steps, I noticed that both mirrors and the TV were covered. There was no way for a ghost to look into this room via a mirror. Was that what had caused this outbreak?

Rap-rap-rap. Silence. *Rap-rap-rap-rap-rap.* I stood on the landing at the top of the stairs by the covered mirror while my "brave" sister lingered at the bottom of the stairs, gazing up at me in anxiety.

There was no way this was the neighbors. I was covered in goose bumps and trembling slightly, though my sixth sense told me that this ghost wasn't going to harm me physically. But I was puzzled and upset by the manifestation. How had the spirit gotten through the wards I'd set up yesterday? Nothing should have made it through those wards.

I addressed the knocking. "You need to leave now," I said sternly. "*She* is not ready for you." I gestured toward my skulking sister, who stood shaking on the lower landing. "She doesn't understand."

The knocking increased, and I could feel the ghost's frustration flowing out to me from the wall behind the mirror. Clearly it did not like my message.

"I know, I know," I said soothingly. "I'm sorry. But she just isn't ready for this yet."

As I spoke I took a few agitated steps around the small space between the top of the staircase and the bed, listening in my mind to what the ghost was feeling as the random rapping continued. How to convince this spirit to leave? I wasn't sure. I'd never met anything so determined to stay before. Usually my mere presence calmed spirits down. This persistent behavior was unique in my experience.

SHAVE AND A HAIRCUT

I turned back to face the shrouded mirror and continued: "We are not here to harm you. We acknowledge you. But my sister needs to sleep, so you need to be quiet now. She isn't ready for this."

The rapping continued unabated.

"Get my spray bottle," I commanded my sister. She raced away to the bathroom and brought back the spray bottle I kept full of scented water used to lighten the atmosphere in places where I stayed. Then she rapidly retreated down the stairs.

I sprayed the room as the random rapping continued behind me, sometimes fast, sometimes slow. I kept up my dialogue, telling the spirit that I wanted it to leave because it was scaring my sister. The rapping slowed, stopped. Then, to my chagrin, it started again. I touched the wall briefly with my hand and reinforced my message. The rapping continued.

Why wasn't this working? I stood back and looked at the wall in frustration. What should I do now? I addressed the spirit again, and as I spoke, cool shimmering air almost like a translucent mist slowly formed around my body. The ghost's energy wavered in front of my eyes like the cold version of a heat haze. My breath crystallized as it left my mouth and nostrils.

"Do you see the mist?" I asked my wide-eyed sister. She stood about halfway up the stairs, clutching the railing with white-knuckled hands. The light from the bedside lamp shone directly on her face as she shrugged. Obviously this moment was not for her.

My heart was thumping, but I forced myself to remain calm. The spirit was all around my body now but made no attempt to violate my person. I wouldn't let it into my mind, and it seemed to know that. My crystallized breath added to the ghostly mist surrounding me. The spirit kept rapping randomly at the wall by the mirror even as it manifested around me. There was no way I was uncovering the mirror, I thought. Like it or not, I wasn't going there. The ghost could deal with me directly.

"You have to stop this," I said again. The rapping continued, and I felt the force of the emotion behind it. No. The ghost wasn't going to stop.

"We were talking about the ghost this afternoon," my sister said nervously, staring at me. "Your nephew wanted to invite the ghost to come home with us and I said no, the ghost lived here."

I absorbed this new data. So in a sense, my sister and my nephew had invited the ghost—I refused to give it a name, which I sensed would strengthen it—into the suite. Which was why my wards hadn't worked. My sister's supernatural gifts are as strong as my own, and my nephew quite probably has them too. And since we'd spent the entire trip protecting him so that he wouldn't be frightened when he encountered supernatural activity, he would naturally think of the ghost as a friend and want to hang out with him.

I made my decision then and there. "All right, we will all sleep downstairs tonight. The ghost can stay up here by himself," I announced to all beings present, corporeal and otherwise.

I moved away from the translucent mist, which dissipated immediately, and grabbed some blankets from the bed. My sister, trembling violently, came quickly upstairs to grab a few more items; we retreated, accompanied by random rapping.

The whole suite remained supernaturally cold as we made our way to the back bedroom. We checked on my nephew, who was sleeping peacefully in my bed. Of course he was. The ghost hadn't been invited into my room. Quite the opposite.

Neither my sister nor I was ready to sleep. Not with an active ghost rapping in our suite. I pulled out some of the tools I use to protect and guide me on my research trips, in case of supernatural encounters like this one. For her peace of mind, my sister needed something to hold on to that could protect her.

We went back to the living room, where I'd thrown the blankets onto the couch. I curled up with them. "I can sleep here," I said, a tad reluctantly, though I was careful not to show that to my sister. The random rapping bothered me more than I was willing to let on to my sister, who was about an inch from screaming and rushing outside in her pajamas.

As my sister settled into her favorite overstuffed chair and ottoman, I explained the various protective properties of each of the items we'd brought into the living room. As we spoke, the rapping upstairs slowed, coming more randomly. Sometimes it stopped for a few minutes and then resumed halfheartedly. After twenty minutes or so, there was silence. Relative silence. But to me the air felt heavy and cold, and I knew the ghost was still there, listening.

"Usually when something like this happens, I leave the place at once and call Mom," my sister confessed as she fingered one of my Native American fetishes. "I've never been in a situation where there was someone along who knew what they were doing."

"Hardly," I said grimly, remembering the wards that had failed tonight. "Let's just say I'm in training."

"Maybe we should all sleep in the car," my sister said, half joking and half serious. I wasn't sure that was a good idea, considering that we were currently parked in a major city.

My sister was fingering a crow fetish as she spoke. I pulled up a description of it on my iPad and handed it to her to read. She scanned it intently. "So," my sister remarked, glancing up from the screen to look at me, "it says here: 'They are wonderful for psychic protection and will literally mob together to drive off negative energy from those they care for.'"

BANG!

The wall shook with the angry knock that came from halfway down the staircase. I jumped in shock when I heard the noise and felt the stab of rage that accompanied it. It felt as if the ghost was trying to break down the wall. It had been silent for several minutes, but now it was making its displeasure felt in no uncertain terms. Following the angry bang, the rapping returned, fierce and full force

"It's okay," I called at once to the ghost. "No one is driving you away. We know this is your home."

Silence followed my remark. It was a listening silence.

After another fifteen minutes of talking, my sister said. "I think he's gone now. We can go to bed."

Cold air caressed my skin, and I gave my sister a disbelieving stare. *Really, Sis? Can't you feel the ghost? It's still here.* Then I realized that my sister was so upset by the rapping sound that she was ignoring the less-direct signs of the ghost's presence. Or perhaps she thought he had quieted down enough for us to go to bed in peace.

I nodded in agreement, noticing her reluctance to leave my presence. I wondered if she was afraid that the ghost would return if she were alone and try to communicate with her again. The thought was enough to freak me out. After all, my sister didn't know how to talk to him. I said, "If you want, I can sleep on the floor in my room instead of here on the couch." I did not say that I'd prefer it that way. I wasn't too keen myself on standing guard out here with an active ghost in the room. But I would if I had to. Fortunately for my peace of mind, my sister agreed at once. I could tell it made her feel better to have me stay with her and my nephew. She shot out of the chair and nearly ran toward the back bedroom. I gathered up the blankets and followed her.

When I stepped into the room, I found my sister wrapped protectively around her son, a little ball of fear and anxiety crouching as far from the door as she could get. This left a huge space on the bed, on the side facing the door. (*Typical; let big sister handle it!*) Well, I thought, at least there's plenty of room for me on the bed! And it beat sleeping on the floor. I lay down, and my nephew snuggled between us without waking up.

The whole house pulsed with tension, and I jumped at every noise, knowing the ghost was still active. I'd left the door partially open and could see the lights I'd left on in the living room and hallway. That open door frightened me. The ghost had come right through the defenses I'd put on the outer walls. What could prevent it from coming through that gap?

I lay awake for an hour, tense as a rod. Finally my sister stirred and turned over. I glanced at her across my calmly sleeping nephew and saw her eyes were wide open. That's when I realized what was happening. My sister's fear and awareness were feeding the spirit. That's why it wasn't going away. She was the open channel. Her connection to the ghost was feeding it strength, calling it to her at the very same time that I was trying to calm it down and put it to back to sleep! Talk about working at cross-purposes!

To confirm my theory, I asked her how she was doing. She said, "My mind is churning. I can't stop thinking about the ghost."

Confirmation. I knew I was right.

I said sternly: "Stop that. I want you to think of twenty happy things you've done over the past year. Right now!"

I was using the same no-nonsense tone I'd taken with the ghost. And it worked. My sister stirred restlessly and then settled down beside her son and cuddled him close. About a minute later I felt the conduit between my sister and the ghost shut as she turned her attention away from him. Immediately the room felt warmer. My sister started to relax, and her breathing settled into a faint snore as she fell asleep.

I turned over onto my back and gazed up toward the dark ceiling. Now that we weren't working at cross-purposes, I could probably do something about the ghost. Dropping my gaze to the faint glow from the face of the alarm clock on the bureau at the far side of the room, I set to work, calling on all my resources to guard the room we were in and make it safe.

After a few minutes I felt the ghost touch my mind, seeking a new conduit to give it strength. I shoved it away. No! The spirit fled back upstairs, and I raised new wards around the room, stronger than any I had made before. I was working more by instinct than anything else. I was going to need some new training if . . . no, wrong word . . . *once* I got us through this situation intact.

At 1:30 a.m. my nephew woke up, confused by his new surroundings and needing the bathroom. My sister made light of the situation, telling him she would explain in the morning. I escorted him to the bathroom. I didn't want him wandering that haunted suite alone. I waited at the door until he finished and then sent him back to bed.

When I reentered the bedroom, I closed the door behind me. I didn't like that partially open door. I knew that spirits aren't contained by normal walls and doors, so the closed door was merely symbolic. My way of telling the ghost: "You are not allowed in here."

My sister and nephew rapidly settled back into a restless sleep, but I stayed awake, extending my work into the rest of the suite once I was sure the bedroom was secure.

When the hotel staff told us about the ghost, they called it a friendly ghost who played little tricks on people—stealing items and making them reappear in strange places, rapping playfully on the walls, filling bathtubs with warm water.

My instinct about this particular haunting told me that the way to ease the situation was not by forcibly driving out the spirit. The best way to calm this would be to fill the whole suite with light and joy and playfulness. Filling my mind with good things, I sent all those good feelings into the suite, hoping it would do some good.

The minutes ticked slowly past. I couldn't sleep. It was one of the longest nights of my life. Without my glasses, I couldn't read the clock. I just stared at the faintly glowing rectangle from its digital face and occasionally reinforced the wards. I jumped at every noise, no matter how faint, that came from the outer suite. And I urgently wished for dawn.

Sometime in the middle of the night—probably about 4 a.m.—the air in the suite shifted. I knew instantly that the ghost had withdrawn and we were alone. Or as alone as anyone ever can be in a haunted hotel. I relaxed—but not much—and rolled over to get a few minutes of sleep myself, since I had to drive to Atlanta in the morning. I only slept for forty-five minutes before anxiety awakened me. I watched the glowing rectangle of the clock face until the faint light of early morning came through the shades.

I rose with first light and walked through the suite, top to bottom, removing the covers from the mirrors upstairs and clearing the air. Everything was fine. The hotel was still haunted, but the ghost wasn't active in our suite at the moment. Thank goodness

By the time I returned to the back bedroom, my little nephew was up and raring to go. My sister was groggy and tired. I told her the suite was safe and gave her a brief lecture on the ways to shut off the connection she had inadvertently established with the ghost so it wouldn't bother us again. Then I went to monitor my little nephew as he ran about the living room.

My nephew was playing with his toys when my sister staggered into the living room and dropped heavily into her favorite chair. We were just discussing who would shower first when several raps sounded on the far wall. My sister looked up in alarm, and my nephew looked up with great interest. "Is that the ghost?" he asked.

"Yes," my sister said, glancing at me. I gave her a warning look, and she instantly changed the subject back to the morning's schedule, ignoring the rapping. Disappointed by her lack of response, the ghostly rapping stopped.

My sister got first dibs on the shower, so my nephew and I started packing his belongings, since we were scheduled to depart after breakfast. My nephew hauled his small suitcase to the top of the steps beside the now-uncovered mirror where most of the action had taken place last night. We started packing toys into the various compartments as we chatted about this and that.

Suddenly, a serious of deliberate, playful raps sounded from the wall behind us. *Rap. Rap-rap. Rap. Rap.*

I immediately recognized the rhythm. It was "Shave and a Haircut," a popular seven-note couplet used at the end of comedy routines. The proper response would be two answering raps, which stood for "two bits." Two bits was a nickname for twenty-five cents, once the cost of a shave and a haircut. It was tempting, but I did not respond to the rapping. I didn't want to encourage the ghost, now that things had calmed down.

My nephew's head shot up. "Is that the ghost?" he asked, wide eyed.

"Yes," I said and immediately asked him about one of the toys he'd forgotten to put in the case. As he turned his attention to more important matters (at least to a five-year-old), I shook my head wryly. I'd been sending joyful energy out into the suite all last night. It sounded as if someone had gotten the message.

We left the suite an hour later without hearing any more rapping. The ghost had sent us his final message. Shave and a haircut . . .

It wasn't until I reached my own home two days that I gently knocked twice on my own walls in response: two bits.

5

The Ferryman

MACON

It was a muggy summer evening, he was tired, and the whole dad-blamed world was against him. Well, perhaps he was exaggerating a bit, the rider acknowledged with a faint grin, but that's what it felt like.

The rider brushed a weary hand across his forehead, trying to push the sweat out of his eyes. He strained forward, hoping to catch a glimpse of the Ocmulgee River in the growing dusk. Once he was across the river, it was only a short distance to the little town of Macon that had grown up around the inn where he and his brother had stayed—what was it, two, three years ago?

That self-same inn was where he would meet his brother again this evening, if the wretched horse would just get him there! The rider cursed the man who sold him the horse. He'd said it was a thoroughbred, but the old nag wouldn't go faster than a trot no matter how hard the rider kicked it.

The heat made his shirt stick to his body and his coat stick to his shirt. His trousers slipped on the damp leather of the saddle. He'd thought the shade from the overhanging trees would make things cooler, but no luck. It was just as hot under the evening trees as it had been when he'd trotted through the noonday meadow. Blast this hot spell. Blast this colony. He should have settled in the North, where the summers were cooler. Maybe he could talk his brother into moving to Massachusetts.

The rider dropped the reins and grabbed his canteen while his so-called thoroughbred plodded down the darkening dirt road. The rider took a swig of the tepid water. It didn't help with the heat. Quite the opposite, it sat on his stomach like a lead balloon and made him feel queasy.

The rider put the canteen back in his saddlebag and looked through the dim light toward the river landing, which still appeared as a distant speck on the horizon. His luck had turned sour two years ago—right about the time he and his brother left Macon with that talkative fellow heading Alabama way. The Alabama chap would not shut up. Gab, gab, gab. Talk, talk, talk. Evelyn this; Evelyn that. He'd told everyone in the bar what kind of house he would buy for Evelyn when they wed and how many kids they'd have. It made a fellow want to lose his lunch. The rider had never heard of a chap so infatuated with a girl. He and his brother would have left the Alabama man far behind if it hadn't been for the fat purse the man was carrying with him. The rider didn't like the man himself, but he liked the man's money.

Ahead, the rider saw a glimmer of starlight on the dark waters of a river. Finally. The crossing was just ahead. Now if the dad-blamed ferryman was around, he should get to the inn at Macon in time for a late supper. The rider gave his mount a heavy kick in the sides. Nothing happened, except the old nag walked a bit slower than before. The rider spent five minutes cursing the horse from here to kingdom come while the river gradually drew closer, filling his vision with its strange, grayish glimmer in the shadowy darkness.

The rider gave a great halloo, hoping to rouse the ferryman. To his relief he heard the splash of oars as a skiff was cast off from the far shore. Finally something was going right. As he watched the dark shadow moving across the dark river, he was reminded strongly of the last time he'd crossed the river. He and his brother had divested the talkative Alabama chap of his heavy purse and given him a couple of knife stabs as a thank-you gesture before shoving him into the river. A good night's work, that. The chap had begged the brothers to spare his life (what a joke) so that he could marry his beloved Evelyn. The rider was so sick of Evelyn by that time that he'd laughed in the man's face as he thrust his knife between his victim's ribs.

The faint smile on the rider's lips at the memory died as the skiff approached. There was something strange about the craft. The boat seemed to shimmer in the darkness. In a ten-foot circle around the skiff, the river water looked gray and reflective, as if mirroring a cloudy sky rather than the dark of night. The temperature around the rider plummeted sixty degrees in a matter of seconds. The sweat froze instantly on his forehead, and he shivered as the skiff pulled up to the shore. The ferryman gazed up at the rider. The rider drew in a sharp breath as he recognized the face. It was the man from Alabama. The man he'd killed two years ago on the banks of this river.

The ferryman's face was deathly white, his eyes dark-rimmed with a dot of red light pulsing where pupils should have been. The rider was hypnotized at the sight of the ghostly ferryman in the suddenly frigid night air. Cicadas called from the woods all around, but in the circle surrounding skiff, horse, and rider,

THE FERRYMAN

there was a heavy silence that pushed on the ears and made the rider's head ache.

The ferryman beckoned to the rider. Unable to resist the summons, the rider slid off his horse and walked forward on leaden legs. Each step felt like a mile, yet he arrived too quickly for comfort. The ferryman pointed to a seat in the skiff. The rider's legs took him over the gunnels and into the boat without conscious volition. His horse, as hypnotized as the rider, stepped into the water beside the boat, prepared to swim across at the ghost's bidding. The ferryman took up his oars.

The bubble of silence followed the skiff across the reflective gray water. The skiff glowed slightly, but the ferryman himself was no more than a dark figure to the terrified rider. As the skiff progressed across the river, the ghastly silhouetted figure began to glow from within. The rider saw that white face with its black-rimmed red eyes staring fixedly at him. The glowing figure wore a white shirt underneath its black coat, which flapped open each time he strained back with the oars. Beneath the coat, the rider could see two ragged gashes in the white shirt. One knife wound made by him; one wound made by his brother. The rider swallowed dryly, his hands shaking. Blood oozed from the gashes as he gazed upon them, staining the ferryman's white shirt until it was red with gore. The rider tore his gaze from the stomach-turning sight and looked up. His gaze locked with that of the ferryman, rowing silently in the seat in front of him, and he could not look away.

The rider yearned for the journey to be over, and yet he was terrified of what would happen when it stopped. Beside the skiff, the old nag swam swift and steady, but the rider heard no sound. The horse shook its head as it swam, splashing water into the boat. Drops of water fell over the boat, turning to snowflakes as they hit the frigid air inside the ghost bubble.

Suddenly the bow of the boat hit the far shore. For a split second the jarring sensation broke the spell upon the rider. With a scream he leapt over the side of the boat into the shallow water and grabbed for the horse's reins. Horse and rider made a run for dry land without a backward glance. The rider knew that if he so much as caught a glimpse of the ferryman from the corner of one eye, he would be doomed to follow the fell creature into the depths of the nether regions, never to return.

The rider fled up the bank, pulling his horse along with ice-covered reins. He flung himself into the saddle when they reached the road. For the first time since he bought the wretched creature, it actually broke into a gallop as the old nag strove to leave the red-eyed wraith far behind it. Behind him a hollow voice boomed: "Stay!"

The rider ignored the command and thundered down the dark road toward the inn at Macon, laughing hysterically with relief. He'd gotten away! A farmer driving a cow home hailed him as he passed, shouting: "How the devil did you get across the river? The skiff overturned in a storm last night, and the ferryman drowned." The frantic rider declined to answer.

When he reached the inn, the rider fell out of the saddle, landing shoulder-first on the top step. He rolled down the stairs in a series of jarring thumps that brought the regulars pouring out the door to see what was wrong. The rider lay in a daze in the dirt at the bottom of the steps, gazing up at his sweat-streaked horse. Then the animal was moved aside and he stared into the black-rimmed red eyes of the ferryman. The ferryman's coat flapped open as he knelt beside the rider, revealing two oozing knife gashes in the white shirt.

The rider screamed in terror, grabbed his knife, and thrust it through the heart of the kneeling ferryman. The phantom gave a terrible gasp and reared back in shock as the knife thrust stopped his beating heart. The ferryman's terrible visage melted away, leaving the rider staring into the face of his brother. With a gasp of pain, his brother fell backward and died in the dirt beside the prone rider.

The rider barely felt the hands that pulled him upright and dragged him off to the local sheriff. His ears did not hear the words of justice that condemned the public murder of his brother. All he heard was his brother's gasp of pain. All he saw was his brother's dying face. And when the noose closed irrevocably over the rider's neck, the last thing his popping eyes perceived was the red-eyed face of the ferryman.

6

You Must Come

CUTHBERT

Lt. Charles Murphy was awakened from slumber by a violent flapping of his tent. He sat up sleepily, staring vaguely at the dark canvas walls. Was a storm approaching? He heard no thunder, and the air was dry.

He rose from his cot, only to find that the tent had gone still and silent as the grave. He strained his ears for a whisper of wind in the trees above the Federal camp, which was installed near Cuthbert to enforce order in the defeated Confederate Army. But there was no wind soughing in the trees; no sound at all from the surrounding camp.

If Charles hadn't been so sleepy, he might have considered the eerie silence rather sinister. The sheer number of soldiers stationed at Cuthbert guaranteed some noise at any hour of the day. Someone was always coming or going, and a surprisingly large number of enlisted men snored. But Charles just fell back among the blankets and was instantly asleep, the strange noise forgotten.

Five minutes later the whole tent started shaking and rattling so violently that Charles shot straight up in bed with a curse and grabbed for a tent pole to steady it. The shaking stopped immediately. Charles frowned. This had to be a prank of some kind. He threw on his clothes and strapped on a pistol, just in case the joke wasn't really a joke. Then he strode forth to confront his tormentor.

The camp was silent and strangely dark. There was no light in any of the surrounding tents, and a solitary campfire had burned down to coals about twenty yards away. The still form of a sentry could be distinguished in the distance, but Charles didn't see anyone nearby. He walked quickly around the tent. No one was there. The prankster must have slipped unseen into his own tent. He was probably smothering laughter in his pillow, the skunk.

A movement near the tree line caught Charles's eye. A figure stepped forward and beckoned. In the light of the waning moon, Charles recognized the face of his brother, who was supposedly taking a week's leave.

Startled, Charles hurried toward his sibling. Before he could speak, his brother said, "Charlie, I am in trouble. You must come."

"Certainly," Charles said. "I'll speak to the sentry. Won't be a moment."

His brother stepped back into the shadows as Charles hurried to the officer on duty and told him there was a family emergency. The officer granted him leave to help his brother, and Charles raced back to the place where his brother waited.

The brothers hurried through moonlit fields and woods. Charles asked his grim-faced sibling to tell him what was wrong, but his brother just repeated: "You must come, Charlie. You must come."

They walked several miles, and then Charles's brother made a sudden turn and descended a steep slope to the edge of a

YOU MUST COME

swamp. Charles stumbled over a shadowy object lying in his path and swore. He caught himself on a tree branch and looked down at the offending obstacle. He gasped and leapt away, staring in shock at the dead body of his brother; lying rigid and bloody at his feet.

Charles's eyes popped open in horror and shock. This couldn't be right. He had just followed his brother to this place. How could his brother be dead?

Charles gazed frantically around the swampy dell, trying to understand what was happening. His eyes landed on the glowing figure of his brother hovering a few inches above the murk of the swamp. His brother's ghost gazed at him sadly and then faded away.

Charles swallowed a scream and knelt beside the corpse. His brother had obviously been shot several days ago. Rigor mortis had set in, and his body was stone cold. His clothing was torn; his pockets inside out. The murderer had robbed his brother of possessions as well as his life. Tears streaming unchecked down his cheeks, Charles ran back to camp to summon his commanding officer.

His fellow soldiers were silently supportive as they brought the body back to camp and prepared it for burial. All had lost kinfolk or friends in the war. Then the search was on for the murder. The woods were searched; people in the neighborhood were questioned; every move from the moment Charles's brother left camp was traced. But no trace of the murderer was found. Charles was frustrated by the lack of progress.

He was fuming about it over breakfast a few days after the funeral when Tom, a close friend of both Murphy brothers, sat down beside him holding a bowl of porridge. There were dark

45

rings under his eyes, as if Tom hadn't slept that night. He said, "I had the strangest dream last night."

Charles looked up from his cup of coffee and tilted his head questioningly.

Tom swallowed nervously. "Your brother appeared in my dream," he continued. "He beckoned to me and said, 'You must come.' So I followed him. He led me to a cabin we searched earlier this week and showed me a hidden cupboard we'd missed in our search. He pointed to a pistol inside the cupboard. Then he vanished."

The two men stared at each other, nonplussed. "Have you told the colonel?" asked Charles.

"Do you think I should?" asked Tom.

Charles nodded. "Yes, I do. The colonel knows my brother's ghost led me to the body. If he believed me, he will believe you. Come on."

The two men left the mess and hurried to the colonel's tent. Shortly thereafter, a group of soldiers was dispatched to the cabin to search for the murder weapon. The pistol was found in the cupboard, just as the ghost had indicated, and the bullets it used were a match for the bullet removed from the dead body.

The farmhand living in the cabin was arrested, and eyewitness testimony soon verified that the man—who reviled Yankees—was seen leading a Union soldier into the woods on the day of the murder.

When the farmhand was marched into camp, infuriated soldiers swarmed the man and lynched him. The colonel forced his way through the angry mob and ordered the farmhand cut down before life was extinguished, insisting that the man face trial. The outcome was the same. The farmhand was tried, condemned, and hanged again in punishment for his crime.

As the body was cut down and carried away, Charles Murphy turned to his friend Tom. "Do you think my brother will rest in peace now that his killer is dead?"

Tom smiled and gestured toward the woods beside the camp. A tall figure in a blue uniform stood watching the two men from the shadows. The ghost smiled at them and saluted. Then he faded away.

7

The Bell Ringer

ATLANTA

"Honestly, that boy could get away with murder!"

His mother's oft-repeated complaint rang through the thief's mind as he drove his stiletto into the bell ringer's back, piercing the man's beating heart. The bell ringer slumped into the dirt of the deserted alleyway, blood pouring from the wound. The thief smiled grimly as he searched the man's pockets for the keys to the bell tower. Getting away with murder was the easy part, he reckoned. It was retrieving the stolen money that was proving difficult. His fingers closed around the keys, lying deep inside the man's waistcoat. At last! The thief hurried out of the alleyway, leaving the bell ringer behind in a congealing pool of blood.

It was a pity it had come to this. The bell ringer was a nice sort. But he was in the way, and the thief couldn't let a mere bell ringer stand between him and the small fortune he'd left in the bell tower of the church after the bank robbery.

If only the sheriff and his men had not been hard on his tail after the theft! But the constabulary had been everywhere, and the thief was forced to stash his stolen money in the first place he could find. Which happened to be the local bell tower, where ringers were practicing the Sunday carillon. The thief had hidden in the base of the tower until the last bell ringer left, then carried the currency-filled cardboard box upstairs and stashed it on a back shelf underneath a coil of rope.

The thief waited for three nights, until furor over the bank theft abated, before attempting to retrieve the stolen money. But when he visited the church, the door to the tower was locked. The thief swore several times. He didn't dare pound on the church doors and demand entry, for what explanation could he give for wanting in at midnight? He had no tools to break down the massive portal and no skill at picking locks.

Frustrated, the fuming thief hurried home. He had to get into the belfry tonight. He couldn't afford to wait for next week's bell practice. WANTED signs with his sketched likeness were posted all over town. His senses screamed at him to leave Atlanta, but the thief wasn't going anywhere without that box of money.

In the afternoon the thief visited the minister of the church, pretending interest in becoming a member. He spoke eloquently of his love for music in general and for church bells in particular. The obliging minister gave him the name of the director of the bell ringers, who would be delighted to have a new recruit.

Once he had a name, the thief tracked down the man with little difficulty and waited in a back alley while the man had drinks at an inn on the outskirts of town. When the bell ringer stepped outside for a breath of fresh air, the waiting thief attacked.

Leaving the dead bell ringer in the alleyway, the thief fled through the maze of streets toward the church. The bell tower loomed darkly against the night sky, silhouetted by the light of a waxing gibbous moon. He was almost to his destination when he saw a policeman sitting in a dilapidated old guardhouse that stood opposite the church. The thief swore and slid behind a tree to watch the man. No one had manned that guardhouse in years. Why now—tonight of all nights? The thief knew the answer. There was a bank robber loose in Atlanta. The sheriff had doubled the number of men on duty, and they grew more aggressive with each passing day.

The thief lurked in the shadows, hoping the policeman would head out on his beat. He only needed one chance to slip into the bell tower and get the box of money. Then he'd be out of town on the next train heading west. He waited for an hour, both anxious and bored. He still had his knife. After killing the bell ringer, it didn't seem such a stretch to kill the policeman as well to attain his goal. But the policeman was armed.

Out of options, the thief crept down the street toward the guardhouse and crouched beneath the back window, feeling for the sash. The policeman sat eating a sandwich and idly watching the street. Suddenly the policeman stood up and hurried to the front window. He stared at the church, feeling for his gun. The thief froze in place and then crept to the side of the building to look at the church, wondering what had caught the policeman's attention. At first glance the thief saw nothing in the street. Or did he? His heart started pounding when he spied a shadowy, cloaked figure in the moonlight. To his astonishment, the dark figure walked straight through the locked door of the bell tower and vanished. The thief rubbed his eyes. Strange.

He looked through the side window of the guardhouse and saw the policeman holding his gun cocked, eyes fixed on the belfry of the church. Above him the tower bells began to hum.

THE BELL RINGER

The thief's gaze returned to the moon-silhouetted tower. Arms prickling with fear, he watched heavy dark bells swaying slightly against the silver light of the moon. A dark figure stood among the bells, running a skeletal finger around the massive rim of the bell closest to the window. Then the dark shape started ringing the bells with its hands, ignoring the pull ropes. The muffled, melancholy tune bit right through the thief crouched beside the guardhouse. With each note, the thief felt an agonizing pain strike through his back and into his beating heart with stiletto sharpness.

The dark figure stepped to the edge of the tower, bells swaying behind it, and pointed a skeletal finger at the crouching thief. The thief gazed upward in horror as the hood fell back, revealing the face of the murdered bell ringer. The man's eyes were two points of fire, his skin withered and blackened as if overwhelmed by a scorching fire that burned just beneath the surface.

The thief felt the knife in his hand go white-hot, like a burning coal. The thief dropped the stiletto in panic and stared incredulously at the raw knife shape burned into his palm. Inside his pocket, the stolen keys grew red hot. He yelped in pain and saw them burning through the heavy cloth of his coat, wisps of smoke rising from the beleaguered garment. Then his whole torso was ablaze, and fire ran down from his coat toward his boots.

The thief screamed, but the sound was as muffled as the ringing of the bells above. He rolled frantically in the dirt, crying out to the policeman to come save him. But his voice did not carry beyond his own ears, and the engulfing flames burned hotter and hotter, no matter how hard he rolled.

The thief flung himself frantically down a side street, searching for water. There must be a stream nearby or a water butt. Something! Anything! The burning thief spied a water trough for horses behind a local inn and plunged into it, body ablaze. To his horror, the thief realized that the flames still burned brightly underneath the water. His hair and face were on fire. In crucifying agony, the thief heard his own skin sizzling, and the water in the trough began to boil.

Once again the thief heard his mother's voice in his head: "Honestly, that boy could get away with murder!" And he knew it wasn't true. Not then. Not now. Not ever again.

It was over in less than a minute. The water trough had boiled dry, and a small pile of ash lay at the bottom of a scorched, man-size hole. Back at the church the bells pealed loudly in triumph. Then they stopped ringing as abruptly as they started, and the dark figure in the tower vanished.

Inside the guardhouse, the policeman tore his eyes from the belfry and rubbed them with his free hand. Had he just seen what he thought he saw? How utterly bizarre.

A month after the murder of their beloved bell chief, the new head bell ringer brought a plain cardboard box to the minister. "I found this on a shelf in the belfry," he said. "It looks like someone made an anonymous donation to the church. Perhaps they want us to refurbish the bells?"

The minister's eyes widened in astonishment as he counted the cash inside the box. "How very generous!" he exclaimed. "I believe we have enough here to refurbish the lot, with some left over to buy a few more bells. Hallelujah!"

"Amen," said the head of the bell ringers.

8

Real Sick

MIDGEVILLE

Everyone said that Walker was the meanest man in the South. His first wife died under peculiar circumstances, and Walker was quick to take over her plantation. His second wife left this world a few short months after giving Walker a son, and folks weren't certain her death was natural either. Some of the local wags claimed that the devil himself was scared of Walker.

Walker owned several plantations by the time he moved to Midgeville with his third wife (brave soul), his son, and his niece. Walker couldn't be bothered to run the plantations himself. He liked his leisure. His overseers tended the plantations while Walker spent his days renovating the family home and growing roses in his conservatory. For a mean man, Walker sure could grow roses. Folks lined up to see the show—and wonder aloud how such a mean fellow could grow something so beautiful.

Folks in Midgeville grew pretty peeved with Walker before too long. He made a bundle lending money to Midgeville folks and then calling in the notes. Whittaker, a wealthy plantation owner, took out a note on a sure-fire cotton crop and then got caught on the far side of a flooded river and couldn't bring his goods to market. By the time the flood receded, the note was due. Whittaker missed the deadline by a whisker, and Walker foreclosed on his mortgage just an hour before Whittaker came to him with the money. It was scandalous behavior, but Walker was in the right legally. Whittaker lost everything, and folks in Midgeville were real angry with Walker over the transaction.

Now if Walker had a soft spot, it was for his niece, Alice, whom he was raising as a daughter. If he had a sore spot, it was for Josiah, the son from his second marriage. The boy had a keen eye and an honest heart that made Walker's bad deeds appear even blacker than they already were. Josiah and his father argued often and loudly. Walker always ended an argument by shouting, "I wish you'd died with your mother!" It was a terrible thing to say, but that was Walker for you. Credit where it's due, Josiah did his best to please his father and be a good son. But it was an uphill battle both ways.

Walker sent Josiah away to school as soon as he could. Josiah saw too much and asked too many questions for his father's peace of mind. Things were quiet around the house with the lad gone, and the kindly third Mrs. Walker, his stepmother, missed the boy. When they received word that the college was sending their boys home due to an outbreak of fever, Mrs. Walker looked forward to seeing her stepson again. Walker, on the other hand, was not pleased. As soon as the boy was home, he sent him down to the newly acquired Whittaker plantation to help the overseer. Anything to get Josiah out of the house.

A few hours later, Josiah came home in a state. He was hot and glassy eyed, obviously in a bad way. Mrs. Walker went to his room to check on him.

"I'm sick. Real sick," Josiah told her as she helped him off with his boots. Mrs. Walker sent Alice to fetch cool water, and she bathed the lad's forehead, which was burning with fever.

When Walker saw the boy's horse in the barn, he came storming inside to find out why his son had come home. "Josiah is real sick," Mrs. Walker told her angry husband. But Walker didn't believe her.

"He ain't sick. He's lazy," Walker roared. He raced up the stairs and shouted at his son, "Get up, boy. Get back to work!"

"I'm sick, Papa. Real sick," Josiah gasped from the bed. "I'm scared, Papa. Please send for the doctor."

"I am not wasting money on a doctor when you aren't sick," Walker retorted. "Get out of bed and get back to work!" Walker slammed the door, leaving his stricken son alone.

Seeing the anxious faces of his wife and little Alice peering up through the railing of the staircase, Walker said: "Stay out of the boy's room. He's just pretending to be sick. He'll come out when he gets hungry. I don't want you waiting on him!"

Mrs. Walker and Alice exchanged glances. They knew Josiah wasn't pretending. He was real sick. Normally Mrs. Walker did what her domineering husband commanded. But she couldn't bear it when Josiah grew delirious and begged for water. As soon as her husband left the house, she took her stepson water.

Josiah lay in bed, staring at nothing and growing weaker with every passing hour. At times his fever raged, stealing his strength. In his delirium, Josiah begged for water, but Walker would not let his wife and niece attend him. They had to sneak upstairs when Walker wasn't around to tend to the boy's needs.

Over the next three days, Josiah sent several messages to his father through Mrs. Walker, begging his father to send for the doctor. Each successive message made Walker angrier. He looked so dangerous that Mrs. Walker did not dare defy him. She was completely under his thumb. On the third day she screwed up her courage and told her husband, "You must send for a doctor. Josiah is dying." This was an act of extreme bravery on the part of his third wife, who had heard stories about the other two.

Walker stared into his wife's eyes, feeling uncomfortable. His conscience was nagging him, telling him he might have misjudged the lad. Maybe Josiah really *was* sick. Walker grudgingly decided to look in on the boy. Mrs. Walker sighed in relief and watched her husband climb the stairs to the landing. At that moment Josiah's bedroom door flew open and her stepson staggered out. Josiah was flushed with fever, covered in sweat, with gray skin and sunken eyes. He grasped the railing to keep himself upright and looked down at Walker on the landing. "Papa," he gasped. "Papa, you see . . ."

He pitched forward, and everyone gasped in alarm. His face went rigid, and then the life faded from his face and he collapsed completely, sliding down the stairs and landing at his father's feet. "Get a doctor! Quick!" Walker screamed as he knelt beside his fallen son. But it was too late. Josiah was dead.

The meanest man in the South had lost his only son, and it was his own fault. Everyone in Midgeville blamed Walker for the boy's death. And that was only the beginning of his troubles. The fever that took Josiah struck down Mrs. Walker and Alice as well. They both died within days of Josiah, leaving Walker alone in the big house. Alone except for the ghost.

Oh, yes, there was a ghost. Josiah's spirit would not, could not rest. A few weeks after the funeral, Walker came face to face

REAL SICK

with his dead son at the top of the stairs. Josiah floated in the doorway of his bedroom, his feet an inch above the floor. He stared morosely at his cruel father, his sunken eyes glazed with illness. Then he vanished. Walker reeled backward and nearly fell down the stairs. "Josiah!" he cried. But no one answered.

From that time onward, Walker often saw the spirit of his son hovering in the doorway of the bedroom. Walker was stricken with fear and remorse every time he saw the ghost. In the end, Walker closed off the top floor and wouldn't set foot there for love or money.

The night after he sealed the upstairs, Walker woke with his heart slamming against his ribs, sure he'd heard something. But what? He strained his ears, and suddenly he heard a voice crying: "Water. Papa, I need water!" It was Josiah. Walker put his fingers in his ears, but he could still hear sobs echoing around the empty house. "Water! I need water."

Walker went through the next day in a daze. He had hardly slept, and there were dark rings around his eyes. He dreaded going home, but fatigue forced him into his bed. He put the pillow over his head, determined to sleep. But he woke at midnight as Josiah's voice rang through the empty home again, begging for a doctor. Walker sat up with a shriek and threw his pillow at the wall. The voice continued sobbing. Walker stuffed cotton in his ears, but it didn't help. The words rang in his mind long after the voice ceased.

Walker started drinking and playing cards at night to take his mind off the haunting. He was reluctant to go home, staying at the bar as long as possible before returning home to sleep. One evening Walker was playing setback with several acquaintances when he looked up and saw Josiah standing behind the card table. He screamed and threw his cards on the table with trembling hands. "Look behind you! My boy is standing there," Walker cried, his face as pale as the grave. His fellow card players turned, but no one was there. Walker was too shaken to finish the hand.

When Walker started seeing Josiah at the foot of his bed at night, he knew the end was near. The boy wordless, his glassy eyes fixed on his father from midnight until dawn. Walker shouted, "Don't look at me! Please don't look at me." But the ghost would not leave. A stroke took Walker in the end. All the while, the meanest man in the South kept begging his dead son for forgiveness that never came.

They say Walker's footsteps can still be heard climbing the staircase in the old house, going to check on his feverish son. And sometimes a loud thud sounds on the landing, right in the place where Josiah died.

9

The Lighthouse

ST. SIMONS ISLAND

My sister is a historian, and she was eager to take a tour of historic St. Simons Island while we were vacationing in Georgia. I wanted to visit the island lighthouse, since lighthouses are a passion of mine. So right after breakfast we packed up my young nephew and hopped into the car. We took the bridge over to the island and parked downtown. When the trolley tour pulled into the parking lot, we hopped aboard.

Little Davey was an instant hit with the trolley folks, being the only youngster aboard. He got to ring the bell and everything! I took pictures with my SLR and listened to stories of history and folklore. I was amazed to learn of the 1742 Battle of Bloody Marsh between Spain and Britain, which took place on the island. The British marched single file through the marsh and routed the Spanish good and proper. We learned that lumber from St. Simons was used to build USS *Constitution*—known as Old Ironsides—during the American Revolution and that the famous Methodist preacher John Wesley had once performed missionary work on the island.

The island had a ghostly heritage as well. The last ship to bring slaves from Africa to the United States docked at St.

Simons Island. Some members of the Ibo tribe marched into the water of the creek in their chains chanting, "The water brought us, the water will take us away," choosing to drown themselves rather than become slaves. Their spirits can still be heard chanting around the mouth of Dunbar Creek.

The Ibo tribal ghosts are not alone on St. Simons. A ghostly light also appears in Christ Church cemetery, still set there for Emily who—in life—was terrified of the dark. And the ghostly Mary the Wanderer, wanders (appropriately enough) through the streets of St. Simons Island looking for her drowned lover.

I perked up when the guide started talking about the ghost in the lighthouse. St. Simons Island Lighthouse was constructed in 1872 to replace the former lighthouse, destroyed during the Civil War. Around 1880 a lighthouse keeper by the name of Frederick Osborne and his assistant, John Stephens, shared quarters in the adjacent lighthouse keeper's house. Osborne lived on the ground floor; his assistant lived on the second story. The apartments were connected by a central stairway.

The men were responsible for keeping the light operating twenty-four hours per day, seven days a week. Such close quarters eventually led to short tempers. The men argued, and lighthouse assistant Stephens shot the keeper. Osborne died from his wounds, and Stephens was arrested and charged with murder. After hearing the case, a jury acquitted the assistant of all charges. However, it didn't take long before folks realized that Osborne's ghost was haunting the lighthouse.

The dead keeper never stopped his nightly routine of inspecting the lighthouse. His figure was often seen in and around the tower, and many claim to have heard strange footsteps going up and down the old spiral staircase.

I glanced over at my sister, who had Davey on her lap. We grinned at each other. Only yesterday one of the women working at the museum on Jekyll Island had told us about the lighthouse ghost. The woman had met him once. She was going down the spiral staircase when she heard someone coming up. The invisible individual had brushed past her and continued up the steps while she hastened downward as quickly as caution allowed!

I was impatient to visit the lighthouse. Maybe we'd meet the mysterious keeper while we were there. After thanking our tour guide and giving Davey a tip for her, which he delivered with aplomb, we headed to the lighthouse and purchased tickets to the museum. Laughing together, all our senses alert for something spooky, the three of us climbed the 129 steps to the top of the 104-foot tower. When we got to the tippy top, my sister and I looked at each other. It wasn't that we saw the ghost, but there was definitely something in the air.

The view from the catwalk was spectacular. Not being keen on heights, I clung to the wall and took several pictures of the Golden Isles and the Atlantic Ocean. Inspired by the view, my sister started singing one of her favorite sea shanties, while Davey proved once again that five-year-old boys are scared of nothing!

My sister headed back inside, with Davey clumping down the steps ahead of her. I lingered for one last photo, pointing my camera upward to get a picture of the light. From the landing below me, I heard my sister start singing again, the same seafaring song she'd sung up on the catwalk. My arms started prickling all over, and I felt a chill in the air that made my eyes water. I went to the top of the spiral staircase and looked down at my sister, who was staring at the view through the small window. When she heard my footsteps, she turned from the window, her eyes wider than normal and said, "He likes my singing. Can you hear the change in the echo?" I blinked rapidly. There was no echo, and that was very strange. No, I was wrong. There was an echo, but it was muted, as if her voice was passing through a cloth. I was covered in goose bumps, and I had the strangest sensation that the lighthouse keeper was standing right next to my sister, though I couldn't see him.

By this time, little Davey was around the bend, heading toward the next landing. My sister and I hurried downstairs after him, and I'm pretty sure there were four of us going down the lighthouse steps, although only three of us had walked up. As we clattered around the final bend, Davey slithered under the steps and then jumped out to join us, crying, "We are playing hide-and-seek!" Chills ran down my neck. We? Who did Davey think he was playing with? I knew he was not referring to his mom or me.

We reentered the museum, once the attached lighthouse keeper's cottage, and I walked upstairs to view the re-created rooms of the assistant keeper. My feeling of being accompanied by an invisible presence grew stronger as I mounted the central staircase that adjoined the upper and lower apartments. I nearly fainted when I walked into one room that had a dummy dressed as a lighthouse keeper sitting at the desk. For a moment I thought I saw the ghost of the keeper overlaid on top of the dummy, and the air around me grew colder. Shivering, I hurried across the hallway and found myself looking at a cast-iron toy that I sensed had been favored by the spirit. Perhaps it reminded him of a toy he played with as a child. Or one that he bought for his family. I'd had enough for the moment. I turned away abruptly and hurried downstairs.

THE LIGHTHOUSE

The lower floor was dedicated to historical exhibits. I walked through the rooms, looking at the cases and trying to ignore the feeling of being watched. Then I joined my nephew in the tiny auditorium to watch a video about the lighthouse. Little Davey thought that "video" meant children's cartoon. He was sadly disappointed. The brave lad watched the boring film for nearly five minutes, sitting and fidgeting on a long wooden bench.

I sat down on the bench behind my nephew, and my sister wandered through the doorway to watch the film and make sure her son was behaving himself. She stood in the aisle and fidgeted even more than Davey. She kept moving from foot to foot, shaking her shoulders and adjusting her posture as if someone had poked her from behind. It was odd.

I saw her take a step forward and then to the left, moving past my bench in a manner that reminded me of a person moving out of the way to let someone take a seat in the row. As she returned to her original spot by the door, an invisible person sat down on the bench beside me. I don't know how else to explain it. I *felt* a man take the seat beside me, even though visually the seat was empty. I sensed that the man was *enjoying* my company. I kept glancing to my right, expecting to meet the invisible man's eyes. But the seat remained vacant, even though I knew a man was occupying it.

Davey grew restless and got up to leave. I nodded to the empty seat beside me and followed my nephew out the door. I was all-over goose bumps again but no longer frightened. We thanked the museum docent and went outside.

"Whew," my sister said. "Did you feel the ghost in there? He came right up behind me in the auditorium. He kept poking me in the middle of my back. I thought I would get frostbite!

An area on my back the size of a quarter was freezing cold. I tried to ignore it for a few minutes, but I couldn't take the cold any more, so I let him pass. When I stepped back to my original spot, my back warmed up immediately."

"Is that why you were fidgeting so much? The ghost came to sit next to me, you know," I said, rubbing my arms, which were still goosefleshed.

"I know," my sister said. "He likes you."

"I think he's still here with us," I said, knowing he'd come out onto the lawn with us. Okay, with me.

My sister's eyes got real big. "I don't feel him now," she said uneasily, but I noticed she moved off the lighthouse property in a hurry. I lingered for a moment, feeling the ghost watching us, wanting us to stay.

Finally I waved good-bye and followed my sibling and nephew onto the sidewalk. My sense of the ghostly presence did not abate until we reached the children's playground several hundred yards from the lighthouse.

As we got back into the car to drive to our vacation condo, I glanced across the park to the lighthouse. The keeper seemed like a very nice sort of ghost. But I was glad to get back to reality.

"Good-bye, Osborne," I whispered and started the car.

10

Till Death Us Do Part

PELHAM

When I took my wedding vows back in 1852, I had no idea that the words "till death us do part" meant my death, not Jessie's. This was a cryin' shame, since Jessie passed first.

I knew something was wrong when a coal-black wild foal came trotting into my yard and thrust its nose into my hand, cool as you please. The sparkle in its dark eyes reminded me of the sparkle Jessie got when she was riled. The foal gave me a knowing look and nudged me so hard it almost knocked me down. Then it trotted away, coal-black body fading as it moved. The foal vanished completely as it turned into the lane.

Jehosaphat, I was spooked! I gave a yip of fright and raced into my one-room cabin, lickety-split. I knew who that foal really was. Jessie had come back, and I didn't know why.

A few nights later I woke up shivering. The cabin was cold as January, and I knew for a fact it was August. It *had* to be haints doing it, and I was pretty sure I knew which haint it was. I opened my eyes and there stood Jessie at the foot of our bed, glowing all around the edges like a body does when they stands in a doorway with the sun behind them. I pulled the covers up to my nose and stared at my dead wife. She stared back at me. Her face was in shadow, but her dark eyes glowed, same as the light all around her. I was a-shivering and a-shaking so bad I couldn't talk, and Jessie didn't say a word neither. Then Jessie faded away, same as the foal. I yipped and stuck my head under the pillow.

I had a terrible time sleeping that night. I kept expecting Jessie to show up. I dozed off round about dawn and was real sleepy all the next day. My teeth started chattering with fright when I washed up that night. I didn't want to go to bed. But nothing happened. Not that night, nor the next night neither. So I relaxed. Maybe Jessie jest looked in to say good-bye to me. That was okay by me; jest so long as it was really good-bye this time.

No such luck. I was hankering fer a drink of water a couple nights later and went outside to draw me some water from the well, since we didn't have none in the cabin. I pulled me up a nice cool bucket of water and set it on the stone brim of the well. When I looked up, there was Jessie, glowing in the light of an invisible sun. She had a sparkle in her dark eyes that meant she had something up her sleeve. I yelped like a young-un and dropped the bucket back down the well. It unreeled real fast and splashed mightily into the water below. By that time I was halfway to the house, so I barely heard it. I slammed the front door behind me and leapt into bed. Put my head under the pillow jest in case Jessie came in after me. The whole bed rattled with my shivering, and it took nigh on an hour for me to calm down. If this kept up, I wasn't going to get a good night's sleep ever again.

Fer the next week I slept with my head under the pillow and refused to turn over even when the cabin turned all January cold. Whenever I felt that chill, I knew Jessie was standing at the foot of the bed. I didn't care how long that pesky dead wife of mine stood there, I wasn't gonna look at her.

At church on Sunday the preacher what married me and Jessie asked me if something was wrong. Guess I looked kind of pale and peaked from lack of sleep. I done asked the preacher what the words "till death us do part" meant when me and Jessie said it to each other in the wedding service. You can bet I'd been stewing on that question ever since Jessie's ghost started visiting me.

The minister chuckled and said, "Is that what's worrying you? You should have asked me sooner! The phrase 'till death us do part' means you can legally marry again now that Jessie has passed. It's about time too. You've grieved long enough, son. Who's the lucky lady?"

The minister patted me on the shoulder and gave me a sly grin. I mumbled something under my breath and got myself away right quick, afore I was forced to confess that the lucky lady was Jessie, come round again to haunt me.

I had supper with a couple of friends from church and didn't start fer home until quite late. It was a real lovely evening. A half-moon hung in the sky, and the stars were sparkling like jewels in a velvet cloth. I liked the sound of that last thought. "The stars are sparkling like jewels in a velvet cloth," I repeated aloud. As a lad I had fancied myself a bit of a poet. I wrote some pretty verses fer Jessie when we was courting. I sighed at the memory and wished Jessie was around to hear my new poem.

At that moment a pair of cold arms slid around my waist and I was suddenly riding pillion with Jessie's ghost. I yelped, and my horse reared and bucked in fright. Then the horse took off, plunging straight across an open field toward a nearby farmhouse. Jessie's cold arms held tight to my waist as the horse leapt the fence and thundered through the farmyard toward the safety of the barn. He reared again when he realized the barn door was closed, and I fell off into a dung heap. Up on the saddle, the ghost of Jessie looked down at me with a sparkle in her dark eyes. Then she faded away as the door of the farmhouse crashed open and the farmer and his family rushed into the yard to see what was wrong.

My horse calmed down right quick now that Jessie's ghost was gone. Can't say the same for myself. I babbled and stuttered so bad they was sure I'd hit my head when I fell. The family set me in a big ol' tin tub to scrub off the muck from the dung heap and then put me straight to bed in the farmer's nightshirt. They even got the doctor in to have a look at me. The doc told me to knock off the hard work fer a day or three cause I looked right peaky. I was real tired of being told I looked peaky. How'd they expect me to look when I couldn't get no sleep at night on account of my wife's ghost?

By the time I got home I was in a right rage 'bout the whole thing. Jessie's ghost was ruining my life, and I was aiming to tell her so the next time she looked in on me. I sat up fer three nights in a row waiting fer that dad-blamed woman to show her face, and did she materialize so much as a little finger? Not she! Jessie always did get the best of me in a fight.

On the fourth night I went to the well to get me a drink of water and there stood Jessie, looking as fetching as the day I married her. Her hair was all done up in little braids, and she glowed all around the edges with spectral light. Her dark eyes had sparkles in them. Maybe she thought if she looked pretty enough, I'd stop being so riled at her. But I didn't care how pretty she looked. I was plumb tired of this haunting business, and I aimed to say so to her face.

"Jessie, why you haunting me?" I shouted when I saw her. "You drove me plumb crazy when you was alive, and yer doing it again now yer dead! What do you want?"

TILL DEATH US DO PART

"Jacob Riley, I thought you'd never ask!" Jessie said. Her voice was jest as I remembered it, a deep contralto with a note of laughter in it. I found it hard going, trying to stay mad when I heard Jessie's voice again. It brought tears to my eyes.

"I couldn't talk to you till you talked to me," Jessie scolded, "and it looked like you weren't ever gonna talk to me!"

"Well I'm talking now," I said grumpily. "What do you want from me, Jessie?"

Jessie gave me a dazzling smile. "I want my teeth," she said. I gaped at her. "What?"

"I want my new teeth," Jessie repeated. "The ones you ordered fer me jest afore I passed. They come in the mail last month, didn't they?"

"How'd you know that?" I asked, eyes wide in amazement.

"The salesman said they'd come in August, so I figured they must be here by now," Jessie said. "I want to be buried with them."

"You're already buried!" I howled.

"You buried me with my old teeth. I want my new ones," Jessie said firmly.

I never could change Jessie's mind when she took that tone with me. I gave in. "All right! I'll bury you with your new teeth," I shouted. "But only if you stop haunting me!"

"Bury me with my new teeth and I'll never haunt you again," Jessie promised. Then she winked and added: "Leastways, not till you get to heaven. Once you do, all bets are off!" She vanished with a saucy pop of inrushing air.

"Well I never!" I exclaimed. All that trouble for a set of false teeth. That was Jessie all over!

I went into the cabin, got out my shovel, and stalked indignantly to the family cemetery with the new set of teeth in my pocket.

"Till death us do part," I grumbled as I stuck my shovel into the dirt in front of Jessie's headstone. "I don't believe a word of it. I think I'm stuck with that woman until eternity passes away."

"And don't you forget it, Jacob Riley," Jessie's voice said in my ear.

An invisible kiss brushed my cheek. Saints preserve me, I couldn't help smiling.

11

I Know Moonrise

Mama told me I should never to walk along the marsh shortcut that led from our plantation to the town of Brunswick. She said it was dangerous and I'd get myself killed if I didn't listen to her. At first this restriction didn't bother me none. I had plenty of work to do in the forge helping Pa, who was the plantation blacksmith. My tasks kept me on the plantation most of the time. But when I grew older, the fellers started laughing at me, saying I was a baby because my folks wouldn't let me take the marsh shortcut. I got so mad I told Mama to her face that I wasn't listening to her no more. She gave me a terrible scold and sent me to bed without supper. I was so mad over the whole thing I could have spit nails! She treated me like a baby and I was thirteen years old!

It was Pa, still smelling of charcoal and smoke from the forge, who came and told me why Mama was so scared of the marsh path. "We thought it best to wait until you had grown some afore telling you the story of the marsh path," Pa said. "Yer mama's little sister disappeared in the marsh a long time ago. She was taking the shortcut to the old pond to gather some firewood, and she never came back. They found her straw hat floating in the stagnant water, but they never found her body."

74

"I ain't gonna fall into the water like Mama's sister what passed," I protested. "I'm thirteen. Big enough to walk alone in the marsh."

"That ain't it, son," Pa said. "I know you're big enough to walk the marsh path without falling in. It's . . ." He rubbed his face with a sweaty palm, eyes troubled. Chills ran up my arms. I'd never seen Pa at a loss for words before. "It's the spirit of yer little aunt," Pa said finally. "She comes to the marsh path some evenings and she . . . she sings."

Color drained from my face and my arms grew goosefleshed. "She's a ghost?" I gasped, clutching the blanket with tense fingers.

"Not just a ghost, son," Pa said. "You heard about the Jack Ma Lantern?"

"'Course, Pa," I said. "It's an evil spirit that tries to drown you in the marsh. You can see his lantern flashing sometimes at night. That's why all the fellers wear their jackets inside out when they walk through the marsh."

"That's right," said Pa. "Yer little aunt, she's kind of like the Jack Ma Lantern. After she drowned, her ghost started floating over the marsh at night, singing softly of death and the grave. She's lonesome and wants her family to join her, so she lures them into the water with her song." Pa swallowed hard and continued: "It's safe fer your buddies to walk that path 'cause *they ain't family.* But if you go there, the ghost will come fer you."

I pulled the covers up around my eyes, and my whole body turned to shivers as Pa described the little girl in the swamp.

Pa continued, "The ghost almost got yer mama, back in our courtin' days. If I hadn't been with her, yer mama would have drowned. She was waist deep in the water, following that singing voice afore I realized she'd left my side. I hauled her out of the mud and threw her over my shoulder, dripping gunk and weed all over my new shirt. Yer mama kicked and hollered something terrible, trying to get away from me so she could follow her little sister's ghost. The spirit floated beside me as I jogged down that trail with yer mama over my shoulder, singing 'I Know Moonlight' in a sweet voice that made my body shake all over. Yer mama screamed at me, wanting to go to her little sister, but I held on tight. As soon as I stepped off the marsh path, the ghost vanished and yer mama went limp. Fer a moment I thought she was dead, but she'd just fainted when the ghost disappeared. That was the last time anyone in yer family ever walked the marsh path."

I blinked. He was right. I couldn't remember seeing anyone in my family on the marsh path. Grandpa, Grandma, my aunts and uncles and grown-up cousins, they all used the road. Pa saw realization dawn on my face and rubbed the top of my head.

"You stay away from the marsh, son," he said.

I should have listened to Pa. But it was easy to forget the ghost in the long days of summer as the fellers and I rambled around the countryside after the day's work was done. I sure wasn't thinking about it the day Jimmy and I were caught in Brunswick after sunset. "My pa's going to be sore at me if I miss dinner," Jimmy said. "We better hurry." We raced down the road toward the plantation. Suddenly Jimmy swerved toward the marsh, and I realized he meant to take the shortcut.

I stared after my buddy, torn between speed and safety. I should take the road. But Jimmy was there, so chances were good that the ghost wouldn't come 'cause he weren't family.

Besides, I reasoned, the little aunt never met me, so why would she want me to join her on the other side? Jimmy's head appeared around a tussocky bend in the path. "Come on," he called impatiently. I whipped off my jacket and turned it inside out to keep Jack Ma Lantern (and my aunt) away. Then I raced down the marsh path after Jimmy.

It was getting real dark, and phantom lights were popping up in the distance while the sky was still turning from gray to black. The wind swished through the marsh grasses, all whisper-whisper-whisper. Jimmy hugged his arms around his body. He didn't like the sound of that wind.

We were walking single file along the path with Jimmy in the lead when a bullfrog bellowed beside us. We shouted in fear, nearly toppling into the water beside the path. Then we laughed nervously, clutching at each other to steady ourselves.

"I thought that frog was the Jack Ma Lantern!" Jimmy exclaimed. With a grin he shook me off and headed down the path. I paused for a moment to admire the moon, which was rising over the treetops, making a glittering path across the still water.

As I turned to follow Jimmy, the air around me grew cold till my whole body shook with chills. Out of the silvery moon-sparkle there came a childlike figure that danced and floated above the dark water like a will-o'-the-wisp. I gasped, my throat tight with fear. I called to Jimmy, just a yard in front of me, but he didn't hear me, and I knew he couldn't see the spirit floating toward us across the marsh. My legs shook so bad that I couldn't walk. The silvery will-o'-the-wisp shimmered and grew until I saw a shining little girl in a straw hat. My mouth opened and shut like a dying fish. Puffs of freezing air formed in front of

I KNOW MOONRISE

my nostrils as the little girl drew closer to the marsh path. Then she started to sing.

I know moonrise, I know star-rise; Lay dis body down.
I walk in de moonlight, I walk in de starlight, To lay
dis body down.
I'll walk in de graveyard, I'll walk through de
graveyard, To lay dis body down.
I'll lie in de grave and stretch out my arms; Lay dis
body down.
I go to de judgment in de evenin' of de day, When I
lay dis body down.
And my soul and your soul will meet in de day, When
I lay dis body down.

Suddenly I relaxed, lovely pictures floating through my head. I saw myself saving the life of the Master, who was so pleased with me that he set me free. Now a free boy, I went to school, studying long hours into the night to earn a place at university. Then I saw myself as an important lawyer, earning enough money to buy Mama and Pa from the Master and set them free. I ran to the old cabin where I once lived with Mama and Pa to tell them the great news. Mama stood at the far side of the room and I called out to her, but she didn't hear me. She held a hand to her ear and beckoned me closer. I hurried toward her, splashing through water that came to my knees, my waist, my chest. There was only one thought in my head. I must reach Mama and tell her that she was free. I shouted the words as loud as I could, but my mouth filled with water and I choked. "Mama!" I called, stretching strangely heavy arms toward her.

She reached toward me, and I was overwhelmed by the stink of stagnant marsh water. My heart froze in fear, for Mama's eyes were glowing silver. The world went dark.

I woke gasping as someone pounded me on the chest. I choked and threw up all over the person who was thumping my ribs. The muddy water coming from my mouth tasted as foul as it smelled. I vomited again, this time vomiting my lunch along with the marsh water. I could hear Jimmy blubbering in the background but felt too ill to open my eyes. Then I heard Pa's voice: "Son? You all right? Son!"

I opened my eyes and saw my pa's face above me in the shimmering moonlight. I was soaked to the skin, and my whole body trembled with cold and shock. "I saw her, Pa," I gasped. "She sang to me. She sang. . . ."

I lost consciousness again. When I woke I was in my bed and Mama was holding my hand and weeping. I stared up at her, vowing then and there that I would never again do anything to make my mama cry. I squeezed her hand and she looked up, startled, when she realized I was awake. She hugged me so tight I could barely breathe and scolded me something fierce for disobeying her. I promised her that I would never walk the marsh path again, and I kept that promise.

But after that night I had to leave the rice fields whenever the slaves sang "I Know Moonlight." Hearing the tune made my whole body shake and my mouth taste of rotting marsh water.

12

Ghost House

We'd lived for twenty peaceful years in that big old white house in Surrency, a town named for our family, the principal residents at the time. We were pleased when the Macon & Brunswick railroad came through our area. My husband, Allan, built a store beside Station Stop 6, and we ran our home as a boardinghouse for travelers. Our home was filled with family, friends, and guests traveling to and fro on the railroad. We had a good life, with two daughters married and several half-grown children about the house to keep things lively. I had no notion that lovely Thursday morning of October 17, 1872, that by evening my whole world would be turned upside down by a ghost.

Allan was late coming home that evening, so our daughter Clem went to the nearby railroad station to meet him. I was deep in dinner preparations when I glanced through the window and saw Clem hurrying toward the house without her father. She looked frightened. Before I could go to meet her and find out what was wrong, my boys thundered into the kitchen and distracted me. While I dealt with the minor crisis, I became aware of a strange thudding sound coming from the yard. The thudding got louder, and I heard Clem's frantic voice in the

GHOST HOUSE

parlor speaking in rapid, high-pitched tones to our guests. Then she rushed into the kitchen, face pale and eyes round as saucers. The thudding sound was thunderous now, as if a crowd of people were throwing hard objects at the house.

"Mama," Clem cried, wringing her hands in agitation. "Mama, I saw an apparition coming toward me down the tracks." Clem had to yell to be heard over the thudding. Outside, I heard men's voices exclaiming in anger, perplexity, and excitement, but I kept my attention on my daughter. "It looked like a man, dressed all in white. I was frightened, so I came back to the house. I'd nearly reached the porch when I heard a whirring noise and a wood knot flew past me from the direction of the apparition. I thought the ghost was throwing things at me, so I turned around, but the man in white had vanished. I sat down on the steps for a moment to catch my breath, and wood knots started falling all around me like rain. I was scared, so I came running inside and sent the men out to investigate."

I ran to the window and looked outside. Wood knots were still falling around the yard at random intervals. Several of our guests were searching the property for vandals, but they found no one hiding among the cypress ponds and saw palmetto. I hurried outside to observe the strange rain of wood. It seemed to pop into existence out of nowhere and hurl itself onto the ground. I didn't know what to make of the phenomenon. Suddenly my sons rushed outside with shouts of alarm. "Mama, come quickly," they bellowed.

Inside the kitchen, the pots were overturning themselves on the stove. A moment later, crockery started flying about, and then silverware. "Get the boys out of here!" I told Clem. Then

I remembered that the minister had come for dinner. Perhaps he'd know what to do. I hurried into the parlor and summoned him into the kitchen.

My husband arrived home during this flurry of supernatural activity. The children hauled him into the kitchen in time to see several glass tumblers slide off the slab, followed by more crockery falling upon the floor.

The rest of that night is a jumble in my mind. The minister kept tossing a stick into the hearth to feed the waning fire, and the stick kept sailing back into the room. Here and there, books hurled themselves off shelves. Biscuits, potatoes, tin pans, water buckets, and pitchers fell randomly throughout the house. No room seemed safe from the mechanisms of the malicious apparition. Every few minutes, it was something new.

I don't think any of us—guests or family—got much sleep that night. There would be a lull and my nerves would calm somewhat. Then a crash would reverberate through the house and I would jerk awake, body tight as a bowstring, while guests and family rushed to investigate in nightshirts, shawls, and hastily donned clothing.

Word got out of course. We had too many guests staying with us to suppress the story, and I found that my beloved helpmeet—I could box his ears—wrote to the newspaper about our spectacular haunting. The house was crammed with folks from neighboring towns and villages, agog to see the ghost. And the ghost did not fail to perform. Clothing was scattered everywhere. The hands of the clock spun rapidly around and around its face at a rate of five hours per minute, my husband calculated. Crockery was smashed. Vases were broken. My lovely keepsakes were shattered.

I spent all day cleaning up after the blasted ghost. Between the money we spent on food for the extra guests and the damage caused by the ghost, we'd be bankrupt before this supernatural episode ended. Mine was the only pessimistic viewpoint. My husband was as excited as our children, an emotion I did not share.

We got a brief respite on Saturday morning, for which I was grateful. The Macon paper printed a brief story about the spirit, and it excited much comment in the neighborhood. The lull in supernatural happenings gave me time to get the house in order and take a nap. I was hoping the supernatural episode had concluded, but the ghost returned to its antics that afternoon, tossing things about like a naughty child. Visitors gaped in astonishment as dishes, books, tumblers, and decorations were smashed on the floor. A pot of water upturned itself. A set of clothes hooks that I'd locked in a drawer materialized out of nowhere and clattered to the floor.

About eight o'clock that evening, while guests and family members gathered in the parlor, I marched into the kitchen and addressed the ceiling. "Either you need to help with the cleaning up or you are going to have to give me another respite," I told the ghost. It must have heard me, because the supernatural activity ceased at 8:30 p.m. and didn't start again until morning.

I woke Sunday morning to find two newspaper reporters in my parlor. They'd arrived in the middle of the night to investigate the purported haunting. "Purported indeed," I grumbled under my breath, filling a pot with water. I woke my husband and sent him into the parlor to deal with them. I had work to do. I heard him making a speech about the ghostly events, followed by a whirling clock demonstration, which our ghost performed on cue, judging by the gasps of amazement I heard from the parlor.

After the clock demonstration, the spirit went into hiding while I fed our guests and tidied up the house. I was preparing the noon meal when I heard a faint thud followed by exclamations. I deduced from the cries that the ghost was throwing scissors. I didn't bother going to look. The next thud was heavy indeed, almost violent. I peered into the front room and saw a reporter holding half of a brickbat in his hand. "It's still hot," he told his fellow newshound. The reporter tried breaking the brickbat by throwing it against the floor, but human strength alone could not break it. There's proof for you, I thought, feeling vindicated.

As we ate the noon meal, an ear of corn appeared above the table and crashed down onto the floor between me and a guest. Kernels scattered everywhere as I stared in fascination at the vegetable on the floor. I didn't remember putting corn on the menu. The guests laughed and exclaimed over the strayed ear. I decided to ignore it and helped myself to mashed potatoes.

Word had spread as far as Savannah by way of a talkative train conductor, and a special train for Sunday afternoon brought still more gawkers to our happy home. As if warming up for the show, the ghost spent the next few hours tossing clothes, books, furniture, and objects of all shapes and sizes around the place. To my annoyance, it began leaving piles of sugar on the floor As if I didn't have enough to clean up!

At 3 p.m. the special train arrived with an influx of sightseers. So many people crammed themselves into our house that I could barely move. I was worn out trying to cater to them all, and to cap it off the ghost went into a sulk and refused to perform. I could hardly blame it. I didn't want to perform myself. When

I thought of all the money we were losing on broken furniture and damaged household goods, plus all the people I had to feed, I sat down on the back steps, threw the apron over my head, and wept.

As soon as the special-train gawkers departed an hour later, the spirit resumed his antics. To my chagrin, several more ears of corn showed up throughout the day. Corn was deucedly hard to clean up. The kernels scattered everywhere. Why couldn't the blasted ghost put them in little piles as it did the sugar!

My husband and I decided to remove the family from the house for twenty-four hours, hoping our departure might alleviate the situation. I packed our bags, and we left our house in the charge of strangers after supper. My husband would return home the next day with the boys to help him with the guests, but Clem and I were staying with the Patterson family for a few days to give us a break.

After our brief exile, I began walking back and forth between the Patterson home and ours to help my husband with the guests and the ghost that brought them. But I wouldn't allow our daughter to come home with me, though she begged to help. Some of the reporters were blaming the supernatural happenings on Clem, and I wanted her far away from the rumors and gossip.

I was working in the kitchen on Tuesday when the ghost acted in the most spectacular fashion, dropping items onto the floor, tossing cutlery around. It was chaos. I couldn't stay in the room. I hurried into the parlor where two skeptical reporters were ensconced with my husband and told them what was happening in the kitchen. "I haven't seen anything that couldn't have been thrown by a living person," one of the reporters said, repeating a remark he'd just made to my husband. I glared at him and gestured toward the phantom-wrecked kitchen. "See for yourself," I growled.

The haunting continued for another nine days. It was an agonizing time filled with crowds, newspapermen, stress, and random destruction of property. Finally I persuaded my husband that we must move out of the house. I was worried that all the crowds and the damage caused by the ghost would ruin us financially. We owned a farm six miles from Surrency, and to this refuge we repaired, leaving the ghost to the mercy of the crowd. Our removal disheartened the spirit. Supernatural occurrences became sporadic, dying away altogether on Halloween night. The crowds faded away as if they had never been, and the house went quiet and still.

We moved back eventually, and the white house in Surrency became our home once more. We never knew why the ghost came ambling down the railroad tracks and into our lives— no more than we knew why it departed shortly after we did. Perhaps we will never know.

We still get the occasional sightseer staying overnight at our boardinghouse in the hopes of seeing the ghost. So far there have been no supernatural manifestations on their behalf. One can only hope it will remain that way.

PART 2

Powers of Darkness and Light

13

Pressed

Folks were real pleased when a young fellow moved into the Cove and built himself a mill. He was a good-looking chap, rugged and handsome. Caught the eye of the local farmer's daughters, who were pleased as Punch when he started attending church and came to the local dances.

It weren't but a month or three after the new miller took up residence in the rooms attached to the newly built mill when he took ill. Showed up on Sunday looking pale and peaked. Found it hard to smile at the pretty girls. Couldn't keep up with the jokes the bachelor fellows told around the pump in the yard. Seemed like he had no breath.

"You best have the doctor in," Farmer Smith advised the new miller. "You don't look so good."

Farmer Smith's eldest girl but one was sympathetic to the new miller's plight and volunteered to bring him a basket of calf's foot jelly and goose grease to help ease his ailment. Her big sister had married a carpenter a year ago, and the second Miss Smith was hankering to get herself a handsome husband like her sis. The miller thanked her kindly, but his eyes were so glazed over Miss Smith weren't sure if he really saw her. Still, she packed him a basket of goodies the next morning and took it over to the mill. To her surprise, the wheel weren't running, and nobody answered when she called. Concerned, she crept into the bachelor's quarters to leave her basket by the fire and found the miller lying abed, gasping for every breath.

"I'll fetch the doc," she cried and hightailed it down the lane, across the bridge, and over the hill to the doc's place. To her relief, the doc was home. As soon as he heard her tale, he went thundering up the lane on horseback to find the miller as pale as death and barely breathing. Seemed as if the life were being pressed out of him by a heavy weight. The doc did everything he could, but the miller stopped breathing a few minutes after he arrived, and that was that.

Everyone in the cove turned out fer the funeral. It were that sad to see such a handsome man die afore his time. Miss Smith was disconsolate. Wept and wrung her hands over the coffin. She was sure she could have saved the miller if she'd arrived sooner. Toothless Granny O'Connor, who lived in a cottage on the Smith farm, patted the girl's hand and told the poor lass, "He was witch-rid. I'se sure of it. I've seen it afore."

"Witch-rid?" Miss Smith gasped, wiping away a tear. "Granny, that's a terrible thing to say! I didn't see no witch in that room; just the miller, gasping his life away."

"Witches is tricky, girl. Some witch stole the breath right out of the man. Wanted his life force fer something wicked she was doing. You mark my words."

Miss Smith didn't heed Granny's mutterings at the time. She was too melancholy over the death of her beau to attend to the warning.

The cove was plagued with bad luck that summer, as if some evil force had gained new strength. Pigs died suddenly. Cows' milk dried up. Old Josiah Jeffrey's farm burnt to the ground and he moved away, claiming he'd been cursed. Jacob McNeil, who lived next door, bought the property for a song the day Josiah packed up and left.

About this time, an old feller wandered into the Cove looking for work. He decided to try his hand at the abandoned mill. He seemed a nice enough chap, so folks started doing business with him. It was real handy having a mill so close to the Cove.

Over on the Smith Farm, toothless old Granny shook her head at the situation. Here was another single chap living at the mill. Tempting fate, he was. Granny was sure the witch had used up the former miller's life force when she burnt down the Jeffreys' farm. That meant she'd be looking for another victim.

Granny went up to the Smith place to share her worries with the farmer's eldest daughter but one, who was still pale and listless after the death of her beau last spring. Miss Smith listened politely to Granny's worries but thought they were groundless. Farmer Smith didn't believe in haints or witches, and he didn't want his girls believing in them either. So Miss Smith didn't heed old Granny's mumblings, even when the second miller took ill with the same complaint that had killed her beau. He grew pale and found it hard to breathe. His chest hurt him all the time, as if it were being pressed by a great weight. One day the mill stopped working. Folks went searching for the old man and found him dead in his bed. His chest looked flattened, and his eyes were popped out as if he'd been pressed to death.

A second wave of bad luck swept through the Cove following the second miller's death. Children fell ill. Horses dropped dead in the field. Healthy crops mildewed overnight or attracted millions of tiny bugs. The Johnston farm across the road from the McNeil place failed when a huge swarm of grasshoppers descended on the fields and ate every morsel. The Johnstons sold their farm to McNeil for a song and left in a hurry. It were real sad. Toothless Granny O'Connor shook her head over her knitting as she rocked in her chair on the front porch of her cottage and wondered where it would all end.

Early the next spring, a new fellow came to the Cove. He possessed a mule and a tinker's cart. The young man was handy with tools and could fix anything. Farmer Smith gave him a meal and hired him to mend fences for a couple of days. Farmer Smith liked the look of the young man, and he liked the way Miss Smith perked up from her doldrums whenever the tinker came into the house. When the young man was done mending fences, Farmer Smith told the tinker all about the vacant mill. The tinker eyed Miss Smith thoughtfully. She looked quite fetching in a newly pressed white apron and a pretty flush on her cheeks. He was sure tired of wandering, and Miss Smith would make a fine wife. The tinker decided to take up milling.

The new miller was efficient and had the mill running smoothly in no time. Folks came from all over to patronize the new mill, since the new fellow kept his prices low and took items in trade when folks didn't have cash in hand. Business was booming, and new customers came each week from the surrounding coves and valleys.

When the day's work was done, the new miller walked to the farm to call on Miss Smith, who looked prettier and more

PRESSED

demure with each visit. She baked him pies and cakes and biscuits till the miller started putting on weight and looking very jolly indeed.

The first Sunday in September, the preacher announced the banns of the new miller and Miss Smith. Everyone crowded around the couple to offer congratulations, and folks couldn't help noticing that the young miller was pale and short of breath. "My chest feels heavy," he told toothless Granny O'Conner when the old lady asked him about it. "I think I may be coming down with a cold."

Granny eyed him sharply and told him to place a broom under his bed and put a circle of salt around his house. "Keeps the witches away," she told him. The miller thanked her gravely for her advice, a twinkle in his eyes. Granny knew the miller didn't believe her, so she caught Miss Smith by the arm and poured a great deal of advice into her ear. Miss Smith patted Granny's hand and thanked her for her kindness. It was obvious that she had no intention of following Granny's instructions.

"Fools," muttered Granny. Was she the only person in the Cove who noticed that the plague of misfortune had dwindled away after the grasshoppers ruined the Johnston farm? Granny reckoned the witch had used up the old miller's life force and would be looking for a new victim. Preferably someone who lived alone, with no wife or children to interfere.

The miller found it difficult to walk to the Smith farm that week. His chest ached, and he kept losing his breath. Miss Smith urged him to visit the doctor. "I'll go tomorrow," her betrothed promised. But he had two big orders to fill, and when the work was done in the evening, he wasn't strong enough to walk to the doctor's house.

When the miller didn't show up at his usual time, Miss Smith was alarmed. She threw on her shawl and hastened down the lane, hoping her beau was working late to fill an order. But the mill wheel was silent and still, and no light burned in the window of the miller's apartment. She knocked on the door, calling his name, then hurried inside. Her heart pounded with fear, remembering what had happened to the other millers.

Sure enough, she found the new miller lying abed, gasping for breath. "The doctor," Miss Smith cried. "I must get the doctor!" But she was reluctant to leave her beloved in this state. Last time, the doctor could not help. As she knelt beside the bed, Miss Smith noticed that the miller seemed to sink lower and lower into his bed, as if he were being pressed by a heavy weight.

She remembered what toothless Granny O'Connor said about the witch, and knew in a flash that it was all true. With a shriek of rage, Miss Smith raced over to the mill to grab a broom. She leapt back into the apartment and swatted the empty air over her betrothed's chest. "You . . . leave . . . him . . . alone!" she screamed, beating the air in time to her words. When that didn't work, Miss Smith ran to the cupboard and grabbed a shaker of salt. Uncapping it, she threw the whole shaker full over the miller. The air above the bed sizzled, and the room was filled with a shrill howling like the scream of an angry cat. Miss Smith recited the Lord's Prayer at the top of her lungs, slapping at the sizzling air with her bare hands. Suddenly a big yellow cat appeared, pressing its huge paws fiercely against the miller's chest. The cat swelled with rage, the hair forming a ridge along its back. Miss Smith reeled backward in horror. Then she leapt to the fireplace and grabbed up a small hand ax. The cat yowled and leapt off the miller's chest, racing for the door with Miss Smith hot on its heels. She swung the ax once, missed, swung again, and cut the toes off the yellow cat's left hind foot. Then it was out the door and vanished into the woods on the far side of the lane.

"Don't you come back," Miss Smith shouted after the fleeing critter, her chest heaving in agitation, a flush of triumph on her pretty face. She heard the bed creak behind her. When she turned, her betrothed was sitting up, looking bewildered. His clothes were covered in salt and bits of straw.

"What happened?" he asked plaintively. Miss Smith flew across the room to give him a big kiss. Then she explained about the witch-cat that had been pressing him to death for the last two weeks. The miller stared from the salt-covered bed to the trail of bloody cat footprints leading out the door. "Old Granny was right!" he exclaimed, unable to believe his eyes. "Yes she was," Miss Smith gasped, hugging him to her in an excess of joy.

The miller packed his belongings and went down to the Smith farm with his betrothed. He slept in the guest room that night and stayed home from church the next morning while the doctor gave him a once-over. Miss Smith stayed home too to make sure the witch didn't try anything. She was making tea when Farmer Smith came rushing in.

"The McNeils are leaving the Cove," Farmer Smith exclaimed. "They're moving up North to stay with relatives on account of Missus McNeil's health. It seems she lost the toes on her left foot yesterday in a freak accident. "

"Looks like Missus McNeil is your witch," the doctor said to Miss Smith, taking a sip of his hot tea.

Miss Smith's eyes grew wide. "That evil woman has been killing the millers and using their life force to put a plague on her neighbors. The McNeil farm has tripled in size since last spring, and it's all because of that witch he married!" Miss Smith sputtered in outrage, her eyes blazing. "Missus McNeil had better leave the Cove or it won't be an ax I use next time. I still have that silver broach mother left me, and it would make some real good silver bullets!"

Miss Smith looked so militant that the doctor and farmer both laughed. "Down girl," Farmer Smith said. "The McNeils are leaving today. McNeil packed their wagon last night. Their eldest boy is taking over their farm."

"Good riddance," Miss Smith said, dusting off her hands. "Now, if you don't mind watching our sick guest, father, I'll take this apple pie down to old Granny O'Connor. I owe her a big thank-you."

She bustled out of the kitchen, and Farmer Smith poured himself a mug of tea and sat down opposite the doctor.

"Funny business, that," he said.

"Sure is, Farmer," the doctor said. "But I'll tell you one thing. There isn't any witch in the whole county who will mess with this cove from now on. Your daughter will see to that!"

14

Haint Hollow

GAINESVILLE

Joe Cooper burst into my cabin without knocking; his small wiry body shaking in panic. "Hank! Hank! You got to help me," he panted, falling to his knees and clutching his chest over his thumping heart.

I jumped up from the wooden table that stood at the center of my one-room cabin, sending my stew bowl flying onto the floor.

"What's wrong, Joe? You look as if haints were after you!"

"They is, Hank! They is!" Joe staggered to his feet and fell into the chair beside the fireplace. He held trembling hands toward the blaze as my dog came wagging up to greet his old friend. "I was walking past Haint Hollow on my way to the mercantile to watch the checkers tournament, and I saw the goblin!"

"You dint!" I gasped, dabbing ruefully at my stew-covered overalls with the napkin tied around my neck.

"I did! It came racing across the road in the shape of a black cat," Joe said, his face going gray at the memory. "When it seen me, it hissed and started getting bigger. Next thing I knew, I was looking at a big ol' black panther with its fangs bared. I gave an almighty yell and hightailed it over here as fast as my legs would carry me. I ain't messin' with no black panther."

HAINT HOLLOW

I stared at my buddy in alarm. Everybody knew there was a goblin in Haint Hollow. Folks said it dropped down from the trees and covered people's eyes with bony hands, putting terrible pictures into their minds and whispering darkly into their ears. Once caught, the goblin wouldn't release its victims until dawn. A few folks in town blamed their premature white hair on the goblin, and it was said that one poor fellow hung himself in despair, unable to free his mind of the terrible images placed there by the goblin.

But Joe's story didn't gibe with other goblin-related tales. "You sure it was the goblin you seen?" I asked. "It dint act like the goblin, leastways, not according to the stories I heard."

"Listen, Hank. I dint stop to ask the haint what it was," Joe said in a wobbly voice. "I just run here as fast as I could."

Seein' that Joe was too upset to talk, I got him a mug of moonshine and poured myself another while I was at it. But my mind kept fussing with the problem. If Joe hadn't seen the goblin, then what *had* he seen? A black cat that transformed into a black panther sounded like a witch-woman to me. But why would a powerful witch-woman be scared of Joe? I looked over at my small friend. He was a skinny fellow with thinning brown hair and huge spectacles. He looked as if a heavy wind might blow him away.

"I'll drive you home in the wagon," I said when Joe finished his moonshine. "Your missus will be worrying."

"Mattie begged me not to walk to town tonight," Joe said, rising reluctantly from his seat by the fire. "She had a premonition that something horrible would happen to me if I went to town. Lord help me, I didn't believe her. I figured all the stories about the goblin were jest nonsense. But I tell you,

Hank, that haint I seen tonight was real!" Joe started shaking all over again just thinking about it.

I hitched my horse, Old Nellie, to my wagon and we set off down the road toward Joe's place. I led the talk around to the checkers competition at the mercantile. Checkers ain't a game fer sissies, not the way we play. There was some heavy betting going on. The two top contenders were the blacksmith and the preacher. Tonight was part two of a three-part championship. I couldn't blame Joe for wanting to watch.

We were debating the merits of the two finalists as we entered Haint Hollow. While Joe talked, I kept my eyes on the trees overhanging the dark road. The air in the hollow was almighty cold for August. There was a light wind rustling the oak leaves overhead, and a crescent moon was playing hide-and-seek with some wispy gray clouds. I wasn't feeling too good about this journey.

Two things happened simultaneously. Old Nellie shied in her traces, and a dark figure swooped down into the wagon and clamped one huge skeletal hand over my eyes and the other over Joe's. "Gotcha!" hissed a sinister voice. The touch of that hand was an abomination. My skin crawled with loathing as fiery images of destruction and despair appeared in my mind.

Then I heard the piercing screech of a large cat coming from the back of the wagon. The loathsome hand fell abruptly from my eyes, and I whirled and kicked out at the twisted obscenity crouching behind my seat. My kick sent the creature sprawling at the feet of a black cat standing in the bed of the wagon. I glanced at Joe to see if he was all right. My wiry friend gaped at the scene through goblin-smeared glasses and shouted: "That's the haint I saw earlier!"

The black cat and the goblin stared fixedly at each another. As I watched, the skin of the haint swirled with grayish smoke, and the cat enlarged abruptly, becoming a massive black panther. It lashed out at the evil creature with one giant paw, claws racking across the twisted face. The goblin gave a howl of pain and leapt from the wagon. It scampered toward the trees with an uneven gait, as if one leg was shorter than the other. That was one haint down—one to go. I wasn't sure which haint was worse, to tell you the truth. I glared at the black panther and it glared back at me for a terrifying moment. Then it spoke.

"I'll thank you, Joe Cooper, to listen to me when I tell you to stay home at night," the panther said. "I ain't rescuing you from that goblin a second time, do you hear? "

Joe's mouth fell open. "Mattie?" he gasped.

The black panther swished her tail, leapt from the wagon, and vanished in the direction of the Cooper cabin. Without any prompting, Old Nellie followed the panther down the lane at a trot while I stared at Joe in shock.

"*My Mattie* is a witch?" Joe said. He looked gob-smacked.

"*Your Mattie* just saved your bacon," I said. "Twice! That goblin must have been stalking you on your way to watch the checker game. It got two of us fer the price of one on the way back. Thank your lucky stars fer your good wife, Joe Cooper. That's what I'm doing."

I watched the lights from the Cooper cabin grow brighter ahead of us and decided Old Nellie and I would spend the night at the Cooper place. Ain't no way I was going back through Haint Hollow tonight. Well, not unless Mattie Cooper came along for the ride.

As I stopped in front of the barn, I got a whiff of hot apple pie through the open window of the house. Mattie must have set a pie in the oven to warm when she got home from rescuing her stubborn husband from the goblin. What a woman! *I wonder if she's got a sister,* I thought as Joe and I unhitched Old Nellie and led her into the barn. Joe Cooper was a lucky man!

15

The Old Tractor

BAXLEY

Mom calls me her crazy son. I've told her a million times that I'm not *crazy;* I'm *inventive*. There's a subtle difference between the two that my mom fails to appreciate.

After I drove Mom's car into the river during my first semester at college, she told me that I was neither crazy nor inventive. I was certifiably insane. I was rather hurt by this remark. How was *I* supposed to know that the branch of the river called "the old ford" was no longer a ford? I figured my mom's old Ford could ford the ford with no trouble, so I used the abandoned lane as a shortcut on my way to school. As I pointed out to my mom after the tow company rescued the car from the river, at least *her* old Ford floated. More or less.

Fortunately for my mom, I was taking a comparative religion course that semester, and thus I was able to forgive her when she took away the keys to the floating Ford. Sadly she was not particularly grateful for this act of piety. Further, she became downright miffed when I told her I'd decided to become a Buddhist monk. Make that a *vegetarian* Buddhist monk. Complete with robe and sandals. Mom refused to buy me Tibetan yak yogurt and yak butter, so I had to make do with margarine and Yoplait. It just wasn't the same. My Buddhist piety faltered a month later when I met Katie Brandon. Realizing I lacked the dedication necessary in a Buddhist monk, I converted to paganism and asked Katie to the movies.

By the time Halloween rolled around, I was back in the old Ford and Katie was my new girlfriend. Katie was really into Halloween, and she wanted to have a ghostly experience to mark the occasion, which worked for me. I told you I was inventive. We'd been planning to go to the Halloween dance at school, but I was not adverse to a little ghost hunting beforehand.

I asked around school to see if anyone knew of a spooky spot where Katie could meet a ghost. Low and behold, a buddy of mine had heard about a haunted old farm out near Baxley that some teens from our school had visited many years ago. The boys—who had graduated many years ahead of us—had met a ghost there one evening when they were out for a drive, and they had passed their story down through several generations of high school students. Apparently the tale came complete with driving directions. Excellent.

On Halloween, right after school, the three of us piled into the old Ford and headed to Baxley. As I drove down the road in the growing twilight, my buddy related the story of the haunted farm as it had been passed down by high school students of yore.

There once was an old farmer living near Baxley who was preparing to plow the field beside his house. It was early September, and he was preparing the field for a fall seeding of rye grass. His little granddaughter had come to the farm for a visit, and when she saw her granddad climbing onto the tractor, she waved to him eagerly, wanting a ride. This was an activity they often shared during her visits, so the farmer took his little granddaughter up on the seat, setting her in front of him, and drove the tractor into the field. The tractor growled and roared and bumped and buzzed its way over the rough field, leaving a long row of turned soil behind it. The little girl giggled with delight and squealed every time they hit a bumpy patch. They could hardly hear each other over the roar of the engine, but just being together was a delight to the farmer and his granddaughter.

All at once the tractor hit a gully and fishtailed. As the old man fought for control of the tractor, his tiny granddaughter lurched to one side. The old man lunged forward, grabbing hold of the hem of her dress, but it ripped and the child fell under the front wheels of the tractor. Frantically the old man hit the brake, but the heavy tractor kept sliding down into the gully, running right over the screaming child and dragging her along as it slid to the bottom and then rolled over, throwing the farmer farther into the ditch. The little girl's screams ceased abruptly when the tractor rolled. The horrified farmer leapt to his feet and raced back toward the tractor. He could see blood in the wavering furrow behind the fallen tractor, and he could make out a tiny crushed body underneath it. He shouted frantically for help, and a couple of farmhands came rushing from the barn to help rescue the child. But it was too late. By the time they hauled the tractor off the little girl, she was dead.

The farmer was so distraught by the accident that he sold his farm and left this part of the country. Some folks say he went insane and spent the rest of his life in an asylum, dying within a few months of the accident. But his ghost continued to haunt the farm where his granddaughter died so tragically, unable to forgive himself for the fatal accident that took her life.

There was dead silence in the car when my buddy finished the tale. Katie, sitting beside me in the front seat, shivered and wiped her eyes. "That is so sad," she said. I took her hand and gave it a quick squeeze to comfort her.

"What does the farmer's ghost look like?" I asked my buddy, mostly to take Katie's mind off the sad story.

"I don't know. In the story the boys heard the ghost driving the tractor," my buddy said. "It doesn't say that they saw the ghost."

A ghost that drove a tractor didn't sound too scary to me, but whatever. It was the only haunted house that we'd heard about in this area, so we would have to make do.

Turns out the directions handed down with the ghost story weren't too accurate. I bumped my way along several back roads as twilight deepened around the car. My buddy kept muttering to himself and yelling at me to turn into this or that likely looking road. It was annoying. We were going to have to turn around soon or we would miss the Halloween dance.

We were passing an abandoned clapboard house when Katie shouted, "There!" She pointed out of the window, and we saw a derelict tractor lying in a shallow ditch at the center of an overgrown field. The tractor had vines growing over it and was so rusted it looked like a strong breeze would break it apart entirely.

"This must be the place," my buddy said as I parked the old Ford in the weedy driveway. "Let's look around."

THE OLD TRACTOR

The moon was rising. It grew brighter as true darkness settled over the old farm. There were broken boards and tall grass and weeds all over the place. I couldn't help thinking about ticks and snakes as we waded around the yard. The field was even more overgrown than the yard, and I didn't fancy walking out there to meet a ghost.

"This place is a dud," said my buddy after a few minutes of wandering. "I bet we missed the haunted farm. I knew we should have turned left at the crossroads."

I held out my hand to Katie, who took it with a relieved grin. "Maybe we can still make it back to school in time for the dance," she whispered to me as we negotiated a discarded pile of rotting planks that stood in the center of the weedy lawn.

At that moment, the screen door slammed behind us. We jumped and whirled around to stare at the clapboard house, which appeared as clear as day in the light of the full Halloween moon. There was no one there—at least no one visible. But the porch creaked and groaned as footsteps stomped across the boards and down the steps. All the hairs on my body were standing on end as I watched the long grass parting before an invisible person's legs as it . . . he . . . whatever it was walked across the lawn and stepped into the field where the derelict tractor crouched in the gully.

Katie was clutching my hand so tightly that my fingers were going numb. Behind us, my buddy was breathing heavily. The air around us was cold. Very cold. We heard the old tractor roar to life, though the vine-covered monstrosity in the field did not move. We heard voices—one high pitched, one low—chatting above the chugging of the engine as the invisible tractor moved back and forth across the field. I could hear it clearly, even though the only thing I saw was the old wreck in the gully. Or was it the only thing? Katie pointed a trembling finger toward the sound of the tractor on the far side of the field, and I saw a moon shadow on the ground. It was the size and shape of a tractor, and two figures—one tall, one small—sat on it.

The shadow was approaching the derelict mass in the gully. Suddenly the shadow lurched and we heard the engine rev strangely. There came the sound of tires sliding, and then a little girl's voice screamed across the field in agony.

Katie wheeled and leapt for the car. Her hand was still clenched in mine, so perforce I followed at speed. My buddy followed hard on our heels. I threw Katie in the front seat of the old Ford, bolted around to the driver's side, and gunned the engine. I was halfway down the road before I remembered to turn on the lights. None of us spoke. Katie cried all the way home.

"Do you still want to go to the dance?" I asked as we pulled up in front of her house. She wiped her eyes and nodded. "I bought a new costume just for the dance," she said. "Pick me up in an hour."

"Okay," I said. My voice was higher pitched than normal, and I was still shaking from our ghostly encounter. I would be hearing the little girl's screams in my dreams tonight.

Katie kissed me and ran into her house as if she were still fleeing from the sounds of the ghostly accident. I didn't blame her one bit.

I dropped my buddy off at his place and banged into my own kitchen a few minutes later. My mom was there, dressed as a witch and carrying a basket of carefully wrapped Halloween cookies for the trick-or-treaters. "Do pagan's believe in ghosts?" I asked my mom, helping myself to a cookie.

"I don't know. You'll have to look it up," Mom said dryly. "Why do you ask?"

Mom is going to think I'm insane again, I thought; certifiably crazy. But I had to tell someone what I'd heard and seen tonight. It burned inside my gut and made me feel sick. So I told her what happened at the old farmhouse. All of it. Even the part about the ghost. My voice got all high pitched again as I described the sounds of the accident and the little girl's screams. By that time my hands were shaking so badly that I put the cookie down on a napkin and stared at the counter, not really seeing it. In my mind I was seeing the rusted tractor lying in a moonlit gully covered all over with vines.

I felt a hand on my shoulder and looked up into Mom's compassionate green eyes. She believed my story. I could tell. Suddenly I felt sorry that I'd floated her Ford in the river. She was a great mom, and I was a crazy boy who didn't deserve her.

"What you heard tonight is called a residual haunting," Mom said. "A residual haunting is a traumatic image or event from a prior time that has imprinted itself on an object or location. Sometimes a traumatic event repeats itself, like it did for you tonight."

"How do you know all this stuff?" I asked her.

Mom smiled a little grimly. "I know this stuff because I was a crazy girl not so long ago. Where do you think you get it from?"

I stared at her blankly for a moment, trying to picture my mom as a crazy girl. Then I grinned. I was going to have to ask Grandma about this—but not now. I had a pretty girl to pick up and a Halloween dance to attend. Best of all, the only ghosts at the dance would be wearing costumes.

"Thanks, Mom," I said. "I gotta run. I'm meeting Katie in half an hour."

"And I've got to get the door," Mom said as the tramp of footsteps on the front walkway indicated the arrival of trick-or-treaters.

As I changed into my Halloween costume, I decided that I preferred reading about ghosts to meeting them—at least for now. Residual or not, one haunting was more than enough for me.

16

Nunnehi

I grew up in the shadow of Blood Mountain. My parents died of the fever when I was a small boy, so I was raised by my grandmother, who often told me stories of the Nunnehi, the Immortals. They are spirit folk who live in the high places of the land, and they are invisible to us mortals.

Grandmother described the wonderful dwellings they built for themselves in the heights, at the bare tops of the tallest mountains. When the sun shone brightly atop Blood Mountain, I would gaze upward, straining my eyes in an attempt to catch a glimpse of those wondrous buildings. But I could not make them out. Once after a thunderstorm, as the dark clouds broke into tiny pieces around the mountain peak, I thought I glimpsed a golden rooftop shining in a beam of sunlight between two clouds. But I blinked and it was gone.

"Why are the Nunnehi invisible?" I asked, leaning on Grandmother's knee as she stirred a pot full of delicious-smelling broth.

"They aren't always invisible," my grandmother said. "They show themselves to mortals sometimes. Let me tell you a story about the Nunnehi." She gave me a bowl of broth, and I sipped the warm liquid as I listened.

"A Nunnehi man appeared to my father once," Grandmother began. "My father had fallen from an isolated ridge while hunting. Father feared for his life. He was far from the normal hunting grounds, and he could not walk with a broken leg. Suddenly a tall man with eyes that glinted gold in the gloomy shadows appeared and knelt beside my father. Father knew that the man was an Immortal, come from the heights to help him. The Nunnehi tended the leg and then lifted my father as if he weighed no more than a baby. He carried my father back to the village, eight miles away, entered his lodge, and set him down on the bed. Then the Immortal vanished before the astonished eyes of my father, mother, and elder sister."

I gazed wide-eyed at Grandmother. How lucky Great-Grandfather had been, to be saved by an Immortal. I longed to see a Nunnehi. But it was very rare to meet one. Only one or two had been glimpsed since my great-grandfather's time.

I grew quickly, as all boys do, and became a warrior renowned for my skills in hunting and tracking. The maidens in our village sought me out as I returned from a successful hunt, but I had no special feelings toward any of them. As a shy boy I had been tormented by the same girls who courted me now. I still heard the old jeers in my mind whenever I looked on a village maiden. But there were other maidens in other villages. I hoped I might meet someone at harvest time, when people from all the villages would gather and dance.

A month before the anticipated harvest dance, I left my lodge before dawn, determined to bring home a deer for my grandmother, who was getting frail and had to be coaxed to eat. I wanted to make her old age pleasurable, for she was very precious to me.

It was a frustrating day, filled with signs of passing deer but not the deer themselves. I went farther and farther afield, barely noticing the growing clouds, the hush overcoming the landscape. When the sun abruptly disappeared, I looked up and saw a dense mist pouring into the woods. Within moments it enveloped me, obscuring trail, ridge, and woods. I stopped immediately. I was high in the mountains, and a misstep here could be fatal.

I groped along the cliff face until I found a nook where I could shelter until the mist cleared. Then I sat and shivered as cold drops of water formed on my skin. I wanted to build a fire, but there was no wood in my nook, and I knew better than to search for firewood in this dangerous fog. I drummed my fingers on my thighs, watching impatiently as the mist grew thicker. My grandmother would worry if I did not come home tonight.

Then I heard a lovely voice singing in the mist. The voice sang a sweet song of fog and mist and soft summer rain. It was a woman's voice, and it came closer and closer as I listened with bated breath. Suddenly a girl appeared in front of my cliff-side nook. Her lovely black hair flowed freely down to her knees, almost like a garment, and she carried a round red basket in her arms. The basket was filled with fruit of a kind I had never seen, and the startled face she turned toward me was exquisite. Her dark eyes were luminous, with a hint of gold in their depths. She was a Nunnehi. She had to be. Who else could walk so freely in a blinding fog? I gaped at her like a stunned child, my mouth open, my mind a roaring, fizzing blank filled with half-formed thoughts that would not coalesce into sentences.

"Oh," she said when she saw me. "Are you lost? Do you need assistance?"

I had trouble speaking. I cleared my throat twice before any words would form around the dry lump in my throat. "I . . . I . . ." I stammered, blushing furiously at my incoherence. The most beautiful girl in the world stood facing me, and I couldn't even talk to her! It was infuriating.

"Not lost," I gasped. "Waiting out the fog. Angry at the fog! Angry at myself for not noticing." I spoke in jerks. I couldn't frame a complete sentence. It was humiliating!

The girl laughed. When she laughed, my head was filled with a vision of sunlight sparkling on water. If dancing sunlight had a sound, this was it. "Come, I will guide you home," she said, beckoning with her dainty hand. "Where do you live?"

I told her the name of my village. She smiled, a dimple showing in one cheek. My legs gave way when she smiled, and I almost fell back into the nook. "I have seen your village," the Immortal maiden said. "I know the way."

I offered to carry her basket, and she gave it to me with a smile that almost toppled me over again. I nearly dropped the basket! "Tell me about yourself, brave warrior who is angry at fog," she said with a gurgle of laughter. So I did. I prattled endlessly to her, as if I were a child again and not a man grown. What must she think of me! But she listened intently and asked all the right questions. And she laughed in all the right places. Time seemed meaningless as we talked and laughed in the fog. Far too soon, we came to the outskirts of the village.

"Here you are," the maiden said, retrieving her basket from me. "I will leave you now."

I stared at her, stricken to the heart. She was going away!

"I don't even know your name," I gasped.

The girl gurgled with laughter. "Of course you do. It was your first thought when you heard me laugh. I am Sun Dancing on Water." She touched my cheek with her free hand. "Goodbye!" She vanished, and the fog swirled uncertainly around the place where she stood before filling in the gap.

I did not move for a long time. My mind was a roaring, fizzing blank. Finally a thought surfaced from the dazzling mess. *Fool. You've fallen in love with an Immortal.*

Grandmother was delighted that I had made it home safely in the fog. We ate stewed rabbit and discussed the comings and goings in the village. I didn't mention Sun Dancing. A lump formed in my throat every time I tried to speak of her. Grandmother put my silence down to fatigue and insisted I sleep right after our meal. As if I could sleep. My mind was still fizzing with emotions, but I had no words to express them.

I knew I had to forget Sun Dancing on Water. She was so far above me that I could not even dream of her. In a frenzy of despair, I threw myself into all my normal activities, hoping they would help me forget. Wishful thinking. I found myself remembering Sun Dancing at the oddest moments during the day. An object or the sound of someone's laugh would remind me of her, and a joyful sort of pain would fill me from head to toe. At those moments I would abruptly stop whatever I was doing, in midsentence if I was speaking to someone, and stare blankly into space until the pain ebbed. It worried my grandmother.

I found it hard to eat. As the weeks passed, I grew thin and pale. Grandmother was very worried about me. The medicine man looked me over but could find nothing wrong with my body, and since I still grew incoherent when I thought about Sun Dancing, I could not tell him about my encounter with the Nunnehi.

I hardly noticed when harvest time came. The dance I had dreamed about less than a month ago had no attraction for me now. But Grandmother was determined I should go. She thought a wife might snap me out of this strange apathy. It almost made me laugh to hear her twittering to herself about it like a bird fussing over its eggs. If only she knew!

Still, I went to the dance to please her. People came from all over the settlement to celebrate the harvest in our village. There were girls everywhere: tall ones, small ones, ugly ones, lovely ones. I hardly noticed them. I lounged with the older men while the young folk danced. Grandmother, sitting with her friends, watched me sharply. I could tell she wanted me to dance. But I couldn't.

I turned away from the laughing crowd—and came face to face with a golden-eyed maiden with one dimple in her cheek. I gaped at her like a small boy, my eyes bulging in shock. "Would you like to dance?" she asked with a teasing grin and took my hand.

I spent the rest of the night talking and dancing with the Immortal girl of my dreams. Sun Dancing was just as lovely as I remembered her. There were three other Nunnehi at the dance with her. I picked them out easily, though Sun Dancing said nothing about them.

Grandmother watched us triumphantly from the sidelines. She knew a woman would snap me out of my lethargy.

Too soon, the dance was over and people departed for their settlements, calling out their farewells and promises to meet

NUNNEHI

again. When her fellow Immortals came to her, Sun Dancing bade me farewell and walked down to the river ford. I watched them departing, pain searing my chest and spreading through my body with my blood.

"Wait," I cried. The knot in my throat strangled the word. I raced after Sun Dancing on Water, but before I could reach her, the four Nunnehi women vanished.

I was too late. Pain tore through my body and I doubled over, my arms wrapped around my middle. I felt my grandmother's arms around me and straightened slowly, like an old man, to look into her wise eyes. She hugged me fiercely; face wrinkled with compassion, for she had seen Sun Dancing vanish and realized I was in love with an Immortal woman. She led me home as if I were an injured child.

I was ill for many days. Grandmother forced food into me, but I still lost weight. I tried to pull myself together for her sake, but my mind was a roaring, fizzing blank. I couldn't speak. I couldn't even dream of Sun Dancing on Water. It might have helped if I could dream of her. But I could not.

A long time later I was awakened by a cold cloth on my forehead.

"Grandmother," I whispered.

I opened my eyes and looked up into a lovely face with a dimple in one cheek. "Sun Dancing?" I gasped.

My grandmother's face appeared beside her. "It will be all right now," Grandmother said. And Sun Dancing smiled.

I learned later that Sun Dancing on Water, upon her return to the Immortal lands after the harvest dance, declared to all and sundry that I would be her husband or she would have none.

This was scandalous behavior for a Nunnehi. No one ever took a mortal as a spouse. But she carried the day. Nunnehi warriors came to our village in the night and carried Grandmother and me to their home on Blood Mountain. They arrived in the nick of time, for another week would have found me dead of my illness. And so I married my Immortal woman, to the oft-voiced delight of my grandmother, and we lived happily together in the golden-roofed city on the mountaintop all the days of our lives.

17

Old House

CAIRO

A heck of a thunderstorm was brewing as me and my cousin George trotted our horses down the rutted lane. The wind was whipping the trees something fierce, and Spanish moss blew right into my face. I was sure glad I had me a calm horse or I would have been thrown. As it was, I hunkered deep into my overcoat, anticipating misery. Riding in the rain is bad, but riding through a thunderstorm is worse. Ear-numbing thunder is bad enough, and then you've got the lightning show . . .

I had me no mind to sizzle to death on my way to my great-aunt's funeral. Going to a funeral is already bad enough. I sure didn't want to make it a double ceremony with me as the second. George felt the same.

"There's a light ahead," George called from my right. "Reckon it's a house. They'd probably put us up during a storm."

We rounded a bend and my heart sank. It was a mighty tiny house—too small to accommodate visitors. We trotted up to the gate, and the front door opened as if we'd thrown a switch. A dozen kids in all shapes and sizes poured into the yard. It looked like some kind of party trick, all them young-uns coming out of such a teeny-tiny house. A plump lady and her man stood behind them, all smiles. "What can we do fer you fellers?" the man called jovially.

"We was looking fer shelter from the storm, but it don't look like ya got the room," I replied. "Is there a place nearby where we can put up fer the night?"

The man's face lost its jolly look. "There's the big house about a mile down, mister, but no one lives there on account of the haints. You'd best bide here with us fer the night. We can give you a blanket by the fire."

"You'd be mighty welcome," said the lady of the manor. The kids gave a cheer that rocked me in my saddle. I couldn't see us getting a good night's sleep among that mob.

"We don't believe in haints," George drawled from his horse. "And we don't want to put you to no trouble. We'll head down to the big house fer the evening." I could tell he was thinking the same as me.

The man and his lady looked glum. I could tell they really were scared of them haints. The kids got all solemn, and the littlest one started to cry. Her mama picked up the child and set her on a hip.

"As you wish, mister," her husband said gravely. "But if things don't work out fer you over there, jest you come along to our place. We'll look after you a treat."

"Thank you," I said, tipping my hat to the lady.

We rode off, and I put my horse into a canter when I heard a growl of thunder in the distance. I didn't want to get stuck in the rain. We raced down the lane, trying to outrun the storm. We made it too, by the skin of our teeth.

The wind was howling and the trees were rattling like bones as we swept into the overgrown yard of a big house. It was a pillared, ivy-covered plantation house; but the windows were cracked, the roof sagged, and the weeds in the yard were up to my horse's knees. Still, it would be dry inside, and we could make a small fire in one of the hearths. There was a dilapidated stable in the back, and George aimed his horse in that direction.

We got our horses settled into a couple of stalls and then raced the storm into the house. Lightning crashed into a tree less than a hundred yards away, and thunder nearly deafened us as the heavens opened up on us and our saddlebags. We charged into the withered mansion, soaked clean through, and paused to catch our breath.

It was sure creepy in the big house. We'd entered a cavernous kitchen, all doom and gloom in the dim storm light. I looked around the room doubtfully as my clothes drip-dried. It smelled like grave dust and mildew. The air was so thick with cobwebs and grime that the inside of my nose itched.

A big wooden table took up the center of the space, with rotting chairs surrounding it. There were wood counters and a sink with a pump. Splintered shelves were filled with mildewed jars and cans. A huge hearth gaped darkly at the far end of the room—all hungry black iron and ashes. A narrow door led to the hallway and the rest of the mansion.

"We could build a fire and make coffee." I had to bellow the words to be heard above the raging storm. George nodded and grabbed a few logs from a dusty wood box beside an open door leading to the hall. The little fire did nothing to expel the gloom, but the smell of the coffee warmed my spirits. I opened the saddlebags and produced dried meat and vittles fer us to chew while we dried off.

George, tearing wolfishly at a loaf of bread, gestured suddenly toward the woodpile in the corner. "Where'd that cat come from?" he asked. I looked where he pointed. A pair of evil-looking green eyes in a whiskered black face looked back at me. A shiver danced along my skin. I rubbed my still-damp arms and hitched my chair closer to the flames. The mysterious black cat yawned, showing wickedly pointed teeth and a blood-red tongue.

"He must have been here the whole time," I lied, knowing full well that the wood box had not contained a cat a moment ago.

"Rubbish," George said around his bread.

"Must be a haint," I said, trying to hide my shudder.

"Don't be a donkey, Jim-boy," George said. "There ain't no such thing as haints. Shoo!" He picked up a rotting piece of wood and threw it at the cat. The cat wasn't there. I saw a movement in the opposite corner of the hearth. The cat sat insolently licking its paw with that blood-red tongue. It blinked devilish green eyes at me and rubbed the wet paw over its ear.

"That's one fast cat," said George. "I said shoo!" He grabbed a burning branch from the fire and flicked it at the cat in the corner. But the cat wasn't there. It was sitting on the woodpile, leg raised as it licked its rear end. The insult was obvious, even to a non–cat person like George.

I sat deeper in my chair and watched George harass the cat. He'd lunge toward one corner with his branch, and the cat would appear in the opposite corner. Back and forth; back and forth.

George's face turned bright red beneath his beard. The cat was insolent and smug in a feline fashion that infuriated George. It would have been funny but for the supernatural aspect of the game. This was not a normal cat. My clothes were steaming nicely from the heat of the fire, but my skin was ice cold.

"Stop it," I said sharply when George pulled out his six-shooter. "Leave the derned cat alone."

But George was mad clean through. He fired point-blank at that black cat, first in one corner of the hearth and then the other. They went back and forth six times afore George ran out of bullets. By this time the cat was twice as large as it was when the game started. It swished its tail at George and then turned its head and winked at me.

Then the cat stood up and bared its teeth in a hiss that filled the whole kitchen. At the sound of a low wail coming from behind us, I whipped around and saw a little skeleton standing in the hall door. It was all glowing bones and grisly pieces of skin rotting off a tiny frame. The skeleton was the same size as the neighbor's tiny child that had cried because we were going to the haunted house. It had a blanket clutched in one skeletal hand, and a flour-stained apron was tied around its small waist.

The grisly little specter started to cry. The black cat yowled at the sound and sprang over George to get to the little skeleton. George knocked over a chair in his haste to get away. The cat stood between me and the baby skeleton. The tiny specter reached a rotting, bony hand toward the cat, and I saw a withered piece of flesh fall off its pinky finger.

It was too much. I screamed and plunged into the rain, George at my heels. We left everything: food, saddlebags, horses. We ran through the downpour until we came to the small shack a mile down the road. George pounded on the wall while I rattled the doorknob. A moment later the door

OLD HOUSE

was wrenched open and I looked into the unsurprised face of the lord of the shack. His lady stood behind him, children clustered round.

"I knew you'd be back," he said and stood aside to let us in. The lady of the house gave us blankets and poured some hot tea. We huddled beside the fire, surrounded by wide-eyed children. I glanced at the tiny girl child and shuddered, remembering the tiny specter that was just her size. Beside me, George gave a yelp when he saw a yellow cat lying on a kitchen stool.

When we were warm and dry, we told the patient family what happened to us at the house. After hearing our tale the man said, "It was long afore our time when folks lived in that big house. According to folks in town, the owner was trading in Savannah when fever swept through the plantation. Killed the slaves, killed the wife. The only ones left alive were the two-year-old son of the plantation owner and his pet cat. The boy crawled into the flour bin wearing nothing but his dead mother's apron and ate flour until it was gone. He starved to death afore his papa got home. The plantation owner found the tiny skeleton in the flour bin, wearing his mother's flour-stained apron, with the cat still guarding him. Boy and cat have haunted the old house ever since."

I didn't want to go back there, but we'd have to get our horses and saddlebags in the morning. I slept among a crowd of smelly children and gave thanks fer every acrid odor, 'cause it meant everyone around me was alive and well. In the morning George and I grabbed our things from the house and headed north as fast as our horses would carry us, leaving the little ghost and his pet cat far behind.

18

Isabella

TALBOT COUNTY

Isabella was always a little strange. Where Mildred and I were fair, Isabella—the middle sister—was tall and broad, with dark shaggy hair and bushy eyebrows. When she smiled, her incisors were pointed like those of a dog or a cat. She had a wicked smile that gave strangers the shivers.

Our mama was widowed at the age of thirty-seven, so my elder brother, Joel, helped run the farm while I assisted Mama with the house. Our family was well-to-do. We had sixteen slaves working for us, and the farm had a wide variety of livestock and horses. We even had a fancy barouche and a large library that was Mama's pride and joy. I didn't care for reading myself. I preferred to bake and take long walks outdoors. Isabella more than made up for my lack of interest in the library.

Isabella spent much of her time reading books on the supernatural and mooning about. As she grew older she had trouble sleeping at night. Whenever the moon rose high and shone through the bedroom window, Isabella grew restless, tossing and turning as if in great pain. Sometimes I would hear her through the wall—for her room adjoined my own—and would get up to tend her. We tried hot milk at bedtime and a variety of herbal cures; we even hung dark curtains to block out the moonlight. Nothing helped.

Finally Mama took Isabella to the doctor, who prescribed soothing syrup—a mixture containing opium that was supposed to help Isabella sleep. It worked pretty well in the beginning until Isabella became addicted to the syrup, needing more and more to put her to sleep. When we took it away, fearing she would harm herself, Isabella's insomnia grew worse.

On more than one occasion, I awoke to the sound of footsteps on the walkway outside. Peeking out the window I saw Isabella roaming through the garden, her dark figure almost animal in appearance as she trotted out of sight. I didn't like the thought of Isabella wandering the countryside at night. What if she fell and hurt herself?

I wanted to confide my worries to someone, but Mama was already worried enough about Isabella without adding my own fears to hers. Joel and Mildred were away at school for the winter, so I couldn't speak to them. Finally I decided to talk over the situation with William Gorman.

How to describe William? It seems too prosaic to call him the son of a local farmer, though this was true. But he was so much more than that. He was quietly good-looking without being vain. He was smart and ambitious and witty. He attended church regularly. He was heir to his father's farm, which was a prosperous one. And he was—for want of a better word—my beau.

I don't know why Mama was so displeased when William came courting me the fall Isabella grew so poorly. True, William was more interested in mining for gold than farming, but many a Georgia man grew rich during the gold rush. Why not William?

Mama was not persuaded by my reasoning. She persisted in viewing William as unreliable.

William showed up on our doorstep one February morning to report that his father's sheep had been attacked in the night.

"It was very strange," he said with a frown. "The shepherd didn't hear anything during the night, but the sheep were dead when he rounded up the flock this morning."

"Did the shepherd see any signs of the animal that killed the sheep? Was it a bear?" I asked, worried for our own flock.

Isabella looked up from her book. "It could have been a wolf," she said, marking her place with a finger. Her dark eyes gazed sharply at William, and her lips parted to show those sharp incisors. Something about the intentness of her gaze made me shiver.

William was scornful. "A wolf? Not likely! There are no wolves around here. Besides, if it had been a wolf, the dogs would have smelled it and barked."

"The same could be said for a bear or a panther," I reminded him.

"And if the dogs had barked?" asked Isabella. "What then?"

"The shepherd would have frightened the beast away," William said. "Or shot it."

Isabella turned back to her book, saying, "I don't know why you are so upset. Every animal feeds on another."

William glared at the back of her dark head and said sharply, "Perhaps. But the animal didn't eat our sheep. It killed them for sport."

Recalling his manners, he turned politely to Mama and inquired after her health. We conversed on neutral matters for a time, then William rose to leave. He asked Mama if she needed anything from the store, since he was going to town. Mama was about to decline his service when I offered to make lemon tarts if William would purchase lemons and flour for us. I was hoping to talk with him alone when he returned with the groceries, knowing he would speak more freely to me than to my family.

My plan worked as expected. When William returned, I raced out to the porch to meet him. As he handed me the groceries, William filled in details about the mysterious death of the sheep. I lingered as long as I could with my beau, but when Mama twitched the curtains in the front room, I knew my time was up. I bade William farewell and went to the kitchen with the lemons and flour.

Isabella pounced on me as soon as I stepped through the kitchen door, wanting to know if William had more details about the dead sheep.

"Yes, there is more, but I don't want to talk about it," I said sharply, envisioning the poor sheep with their throats torn out, blood all over their white fleece. "It's horrible!"

Isabella licked her lips, and for a moment those sharp canines gleamed suggestively. I glared at her. I would not be intimidated by my own baby sister. Isabella backed down and retreated to the library with her book. I spent the rest of the evening making lemon tarts to sooth my jangled nerves.

A couple of days later, William dropped by to sample my baking. The servants served tea and lemon tarts in the library, and Mama joined us as chaperone. To my surprise, Isabella left her books to join the tea party. I soon learned the reason. Isabella asked William for more information about the animal that killed his sheep. She pushed him for details, seeming obsessed by the story, dark eyes gleaming under her bushy eyebrows. William shrugged uneasily and said, "We haven't had any more sheep attacks, thank goodness. Although I did hear that there was trouble at a nearby cattle farm."

Isabella's eyes sparkled. "Truly?" she asked and fired questions at William, one after another, without waiting for a response.

"Isabella, really," I said in my best big-sister tone. "Why do you persist in talking about something so unpleasant?"

Isabella whirled on me with a snarl, teeth bared and canines gleaming. It was an animal reaction, and I jerked back in shock. She grabbed my arm and pulled me to face her. I thought my arm would come out of its socket.

"You know nothing about it," Isabella shouted, face contorted with rage.

I was frightened, but I refused to back down. Glaring at my little sister, I tried to break her grip on my arm. William half rose from his seat, eyes blazing. At the same moment, Mama ordered Isabella to release me. Seeing the shocked faces around her, Isabella dropped my arm, her face still dark with anger.

William settled back into his seat without comment, bless him. He finished his cup of tea, placed it on the tray, and bade us a polite farewell. As he passed my chair, he murmured: "Meet me on the porch." Then he was gone.

"Well," said Mama into the silence. "We'd best have a look at the account books. We will need a detailed inventory of the stock."

"I'll get them," I said, glad of an excuse to quit the room.

At the same moment a knock sounded at the front door. Knowing it was William, I rushed to answer it. I stepped onto the porch and shut the door firmly behind me.

ISABELLA

"The men are going hunting tonight, Sarah," William said. "We are going to solve this problem tonight, one way or another, even if it means we have to use silver bullets." He pressed a small pistol into my hand. "Take this, just in case. And please do not go outdoors tonight."

I stared down at the wicked little pistol William had placed in my hand. It was small enough to fit in my pocket. Why was William giving me a gun? Unless . . . I pictured the anger contorting my sister's face. Combined with William's statement about silver bullets, it suggested something so awful that I closed my mind to the picture.

"Oh no, William! Surely . . ." I said and choked, unable to voice my suspicions aloud. Finally I hugged him and whispered, "Be careful."

"I will come tomorrow to tell you what happened," William said, touching my cheek tenderly with two fingers. He hurried away, and I watched until he was out of sight.

Things were tense over dinner. Isabella had an air of suppressed excitement about her that worried me exceedingly. Pictures of pistols and silver bullets and dead sheep kept flashing through my worried mind as we ate, and my bruised arm throbbed every time I looked at my little sister. By the end of the meal, I had a pounding headache. I excused myself and went to bed early, afraid of what I would learn on the morrow. Afraid for Isabella, my baby sister. The pistol lay in my pocket, a constant reminder of tonight's hunt. In the end I put it in the drawer of my bedside table just before I fell asleep.

I was awakened at midnight by footsteps outside my door. I threw on a dressing gown, put the pistol in my pocket, and hurried into the hallway. My mother was descending the staircase, her attention on the front door. I followed her gaze and saw Isabella slipping outside. My heart sank. Please no! It couldn't possibly be true. My baby sister couldn't possibly be a . . . be a werewolf. Could she?

Mama trailed Isabella through the gardens and out into the fields. I followed unnoticed. It didn't take long to realize where we were going. Isabella was making for the sheep pasture, loping ahead of us on all fours like a wolf. She leapt the fence easily and lunged toward a white shape bleating in sudden terror. I heard Mama shout, and Isabella whirled in midair, a feat hitherto I had only seen performed by rabbits. Isabella ran toward Mama, teeth bared, and I saw a knife gleaming in her hand.

With a cry of terror, I pulled the gun from my pocket and raised it with trembling hands. I didn't think I could shoot my own sister. But Isabella was going to hurt Mama! As I took aim I heard a gunshot reverberate through the pasture and Isabella scream. I fainted.

When I came to I was in my own bed, with the doctor bending over me. He smiled and gave me a drink of water. Then he told me what had happened. William and his hunting party reached the sheep pasture about the same time as Isabella. According to the doctor, Isabella had gotten mixed in with the hunting party, and her left hand was shot off during the melee. The "werewolf" had gotten away.

William's story, which he told me the next afternoon, was different. "We saw your sister attacking your mother. Your mother had a pistol, and she shot the knife out of your sister's hand before Isabella could cut her throat. The sheep panicked when they heard the gunshot and raced everywhere, blocking our access to your mother. By the time we made it to the pasture, it was over. Isabella was kneeling on the ground cradling the stump of her left hand, and your mother was tearing up her petticoat to bandage the injured arm. One of the men saw you lying near the fence, and I carried you home. Your mother was as cool as a cucumber through the whole scene. What a lady!"

Isabella was sent to Paris to "visit relatives." In truth, Mama put her in the care of a doctor who specialized in lycanthropy, a mental disease in which people convince themselves that they are werewolves. No animals went missing in the months that Isabella was gone. She didn't return home until the Paris doctor proclaimed her cured of her mental disorder.

Isabella always remained a bit strange. She lived a long and productive life, but she never married. If a sheep went missing now and again in Talbot County, no one was crass enough to comment on the matter. And my children, when they came, were fond of their Aunt Isabella, who spoiled them rotten. So things worked out in the end.

19

Treasure

CHATSWORTH

She was elderly, impoverished, and tired. So very tired. She had been mistress of the local day school until her eyesight gave out. But the little she had saved from her meager teacher's salary was barely enough to keep body and soul together.

When the cheap boardinghouse in which she had resided for more than thirty years was purchased by a greedy man at the end of the Civil War, the old lady knew she was in trouble. The man didn't care two pennies for any of the old-timers living in his new property. He sent a letter to all the tenants announcing that he had raised the rent, and he laughed when the old-timers gave him a piece of their collective minds.

As far as the new landlord was concerned, there were plenty of people out there who would pay high prices for their board and be glad to have a roof over their heads. And he was right. Soon the boardinghouse filled up with former soldiers and businessmen.

The old lady, who had nowhere else to go, was uncomfortable among the new tenants. She knew that the landlord was looking for an excuse to evict her. And it would not be long in coming.

The high rent was eating into her savings. It would not be long before her money was gone.

On the first day of January—New Years Day—the old schoolteacher counted her money and knew it was not enough to pay the rent. She went to the landlord with the partial payment, and he ordered her to vacate immediately. Mute with terror, the old lady packed her meager belongings into an ancient black valise and walked down the stairs of the boardinghouse for the last time. The landlord locked the door of her room behind her and took away her key.

The old schoolteacher stood on the creaky front porch and stared blindly at the street, wondering what to do. She had no family, and all her friends were dead. It was colder than normal this winter. She could not sleep outside.

Shivering, the old lady pulled her coat tightly around her, tucking a scarf around her wrinkled neck. She started walking aimlessly down the road, the heavy bag leaving welts on her skinny old hands. Her worn gloves quickly tore under this harsh treatment. She pulled the tattered remains from her hands and stuck them in a pocket. She stopped frequently, setting the bag down and staring into the woods around her as she shook life back into her stinging palms. Her mind was a blank. She could not think about the future. She just walked and walked and walked.

As the light began to fail, the old lady found herself walking down an overgrown lane leading toward the abandoned Fox residence. Folks in town never came here. It was said that a headless ghost haunted the house and grounds. But she was desperate for a roof over her head and didn't care if a thousand ghosts lived in the house. She could stay here until she found a new home.

The old lady picked up her heavy bag and trudged through the weedy lane as shadows deepened around her. She could see the weathered old covered bridge looming ahead of her in the gloom. In the light of the gibbous moon rising majestically over the oak trees, she studied the bridge. The boards were warped, and there was a huge splintered hole in the floor through which she could see the water a long way below. The roof was covered in moss and sagged in the middle.

The old lady stopped and stared at the rickety structure, frightened to go on. What if it collapsed under her feet? She would drown in the rushing water below. But she had no choice. It was either risk the bridge or let her old body freeze in the unsheltered night air.

Straightening her shoulders, the old lady stepped cautiously onto the creaky bridge, keeping to one side to avoid the hole in the floor. Around her the temperature plummeted like a stone. Wind gusted through the tunnel, knocking her sideways into the wall as a sepulchral voice began to moan. *"Ooooooooohhhhhhhh!"* the voice wailed on the wind. *"Ooooooooohhhhhhhh!"*

The old lady fell to her knees in dismay. Surely this must be the voice of the ghost! Dare she go on? But she must or freeze to death in the darkness of the covered bridge. Keeping one trembling old hand on the splintered wall for balance, the old lady pushed through the forceful wind that howled through the covered bridge. At long last she stepped into the moonlit lane and stood facing the ruined Fox house.

The wind was even stronger in the lane, swirling around her like a cyclone, snatching at the scarf around her wrinkled neck. The old lady freed one rubbed-raw hand from the black bag to clutch at her scarf, staring in dismay at the sinister old house

TREASURE

with its ruined porch and dark windows that stared at her like the eyes of a hungry beast.

"*Oooooooohhhhhhhh,*" moaned the wind. "*Oooooooohhhhhhhh!*"

She heard the sound of galloping hooves crossing the bridge behind her. The old lady whirled, cold sweat breaking out all over her wrinkled body. Her old heart was beating so hard she thought it would burst. A glowing figure burst forth from the covered bridge. The man atop the ghostly steed wore the costume of a Revolutionary soldier, and he had no head!

The old lady stood paralyzed, staring at the headless horseman galloping toward her at speed. The black bag slipped from her hands, and she raised her stinging palms in a gesture of repudiation, as if her will alone could stop the phantom's approach. Closer it came, and still closer. The old lady's legs trembled beneath her, too weak to run. Her eyes were fixed on the terrible figure, and she could feel them drying in the howling wind. *Please, God, let it be over quickly,* she prayed silently. The horse reared above her, hooves flailing the air.

The old lady closed her eyes in despair. And then she heard a voice inside her head.

"At last! You have come at last!"

It was a man's voice. His tone was one of relief and joy. The old lady opened her eyes in astonishment. The horse was standing now, watching her with dark eyes that glowed from within. The headless figure on its back was holding one hand toward her, palm up, beseeching her to listen, to understand.

"My lady," the headless horseman said into her mind, "in life I was a miser who cherished money above all else. I ruined many innocent people who owed me money, and more than one child was orphaned by my neglect. When I was summoned to war, I buried my treasure here on this land to keep it safe until my return. But a cannonball decapitated me during battle, and my treasure remains hidden to this day. If I had been blameless, my spirit would have gone directly to heaven. But for my crimes, my spirit was tied to this place, doomed to ride this lane forever unless some brave soul should ask me to reveal the location of my treasure. Will you ask, dear lady, and release my spirit from this place?"

The old lady took a deep breath, her ribs aching from her terrible fright.

"Please, sir, will you tell me where your treasure is buried?" she quavered, trembling with cold and fear.

Directions to the treasure poured into the old lady's mind. With the final word spoken, the phantom gave a mighty shout. The light glowing through horse and headless rider grew in intensity until the old lady was forced to shield her eyes. For a moment the world went white. Then the old lady was alone in the darkness, with her black bag and her pounding heart. And half a million dollars buried twenty feet from the place she stood.

It is amazing what a body—even an old one—can do with the proper motivation. With the help of a dilapidated shovel discovered in a ruined tool shed, the old lady dug up a trunk full of gold coins and dragged it into the house, using an impromptu travois like the ones she had made with the schoolchildren many years ago. She lit a fire in the old fireplace and sat eating a dried apple—all the food she had left—while she counted her newfound wealth.

In the morning the old lady went to the bank and deposited the money. In the afternoon she went to the lawyer of her former landlord and offered him cash on the barrelhead for the boardinghouse.

On the third day of January, the old lady evicted her evictor and moved back into her old home for good. Using her newfound gold, she renovated the old boardinghouse, turning it into a real home with proper furniture and servants and a fancy butler to open her front door to visitors.

When folks in town asked the old lady how she had come by her good fortune, she told them it was an unexpected inheritance from an old friend. Which was the exact truth. She never went into details, though, for who would believe her if she did?

20

Hurry, Hurry

JEKYLL ISLAND

I eagerly boarded the red trolley that would take us on a tour of the historic district. I was vacationing on Jekyll Island with my sister and nephew, and we'd heard about this particular tour from our server at last night's restaurant. It sounded like a lot of fun, so we'd signed up. My five-year-old nephew crowed delightedly when he saw the trolley and wanted to sit up front. I perched in the seat behind with my digital SLR at the ready, hoping to capture photos of the fancy "cottages" erected by Northern millionaires come to this exclusive island for the worst of the winter months. Names like J. P. Morgan, Pulitzer, Macy, Vanderbilt, and Rockefeller spun easily from the lips of the tour guide as the trolley meandered through the grounds of the historic district.

We made two stops during our trolley tour, and I quickly realized that both the "cottages" were haunted. This fact was not mentioned by our tour guide, it being a historical tour. But my sister and I knew it just the same, since we both have second sight, handed down to us from a Pennsylvania Dutch grandmother.

While exploring the first cottage, I walked into a cold spot in the upstairs hallway. My little nephew, walking beside me, whimpered when he felt the chill touch of the ghost. We abandoned the upstairs at speed, leaving my puzzled sister behind. She strolled over to the same spot, shivered in understanding, and followed.

The second cottage featured a male ghost who spent most of the visit watching us from the staircase landing. I kept expecting to see the ghost whenever I looked into a mirror, of which there were many, but he did not materialize.

The rest of the tour, while interesting from a historical perspective, remained blessedly free of ghosts. We exited the trolley and thanked our guide, and the three of us headed to the clubhouse for lunch. I was ready for food, and even more ready to be done with ghostly things for a time. So it was probably silly of me to have lunch in a haunted hotel. Still, I wanted to dine in the same room where Rockefeller and Morgan had once dined.

I was struck by the historical feel of the fancy dining room, but I could see that my sister was struck by something else. She has a "gift" for seeing people and places as they looked in the past. I wondered what she was seeing here. When I asked, she described the scene as she "saw" it—how the people looked back then, where they sat, how they felt, what they were eating. It was uncanny, as if she were describing a painting only she could see. It gave me goose bumps.

The food was excellent, the service was excellent, and the large dining room was redolent of the Gilded Age in both decor and atmosphere. It was everything, in fact, that I had hoped for.

Lunch behind us, my sister wanted to explore the hotel. There was a lovely if rather creaky wooden staircase just opposite the bar that wound its way up several stories. Davey led the way up and up the staircase, with my sister hard on his heels. They

HURRY, HURRY

stopped to peek along the bedroom corridor on each floor, while I followed rather ponderously behind, feeling replete from my meal and in no great hurry to explore.

My sister was obviously still looking for ghosts, which suited me. She could hang out with ghosts all day if she wanted. I was content to see the beautiful decor on each floor and listen to the chatter of my nephew. By the time I began the ascent from the third floor to the fourth, my sister was nearly at the top and Davey was already out of view. And that's when things got a bit surreal for me. The sunlight was streaming through the fourth-floor windows, illuminating the lovely broad staircase with its carved banister, empty save my sister, who was nearly at the top already. For a moment I was alone on the stairs, and time seemed to slow down. My ears were straining behind me, listening to my footsteps on the creaky wooden steps. There was a two-second delay between the time my foot hit the step and the creaky groan the wood made as it took my weight. It was very odd. There had been no sound delay on the second- and third-floor staircases. Why was it happening now?

For some reason, as I continued upward I became convinced that someone was walking up the stairs behind me. I heard his footfalls rather than my own. I turned the corner on the landing with an invisible someone following behind me. As I turned I felt a sudden urge to move to the right of the staircase and grab the carved banister as if for support. A moment later I felt someone rush past me at speed. *Hurry! Hurry!* I felt the words in my bones, though no one spoke aloud. For a second I saw him as he turned on the landing and raced down to the third floor, a shadowy figure seen from the corner of my eye. He was a young, clean-shaven man wearing the formal garb of a previous era. By the time I turned my head, he had vanished. For a moment I still felt the anxiety that drove him onward. *Hurry! Hurry!* What struck me most about the ghost was his look of suppressed panic. He sped down the staircase as if he could not move fast enough.

Then time sped up again and my sister was calling out to me: "What is it? Did you see something?"

"A shadow out of the corner of my eye," I said gruffly, not ready to talk about the young man I'd seen. He had vanished as quickly as he had come, and I knew I was alone on the stairs. Had the invisible follower been searching for the young man? They'd both departed in the same instant. I wondered if I had unknowingly witnessed a past event. I'd heard that a former bellman haunted the property. Could he be the rushing young man?

I finished climbing to the fourth floor and followed my sister and her little son into the upstairs corridor, wandering along the length of the building until I came to a door that made my skin prickle. There was something supernatural in that room. I knew it at once. Whether it was connected to the rushing young man I couldn't say. My sister looked at me and pointed to the same door. I nodded. She looked a little creeped out and walked quickly down the corridor. I followed at once.

All this supernatural activity left me feeling emotionally exhausted—too many sensations in too short a time. I was done mentally, if not physically. I chivied my family members downstairs to the bathroom and managed, by dint of sheer willpower, to convince my sibling that enough was enough. If she wanted to talk to ghosts, she could do it alone. Davey and I were going to the beach! Reluctantly my sister followed us outside. She cheered up when she saw what a beautiful day it was. And she was even happier when I told her that we could look for more ghosts tomorrow.

We headed to the car, our thoughts already occupied with dolphins and seashells and warm sand. Behind us, the clubhouse silently dreamed of days both old and new in the warm sunlight of a January afternoon.

21

Resurrection Man

AUGUSTA

I enrolled in Georgia Medical College in 1855, and I sure as heck didn't know what I was getting into. Medical students need nerves of iron. I realized this fact the first time I strolled into a classroom and saw a corpse lying on the table. I almost turned tail and ran for my life when I realized that we were going to dissect it.

The teacher put me and a fellow student named Ted to work on the body of a deceased man in his late sixties. The corpse looked pinched and gray, though it was obviously fresh. I was not looking forward to seeing his insides. But I was determined to be a doctor, like my father before me. So I curbed my rebellious stomach and got to work.

It's astonishing how quickly you adjust to even the most bizarre circumstances. Within a month or so, dissection was no big deal and Ted was my best buddy. Nothing like a corpse to bond fellows together, as Ted said.

"I wonder where this bloke came from," Ted said as I carefully extracted a lung.

"People donate their bodies to the college," I said, too absorbed in my task to pay attention to Ted.

Ted glanced incredulously at me. "Oh sure, some do. But look around, Frank. There is no possible way that the college received this many donations! Look at the scars on this fellow's body. Those are whip marks. This fellow was a slave. I don't think many slaves donate their bodies to science after death."

I glanced up, struck by his words. Then I looked around the room. He was right. A proportionally large number of the cadavers looked as if they had come from the slave cemetery. I lowered my voice and whispered: "What are you saying, Ted? That the college stole these corpses?"

Ted smirked at me and said, "Why else do you think they purchased that Gullah slave? What's his name?"

"You mean Grandison Harris?" I asked, remembering the man I'd seen around campus. He was a nice fellow, though he looked tired most of the time, as if he had trouble sleeping at night. I blinked, putting two and two together. Grandison's weary appearance plus Ted's hints equaled . . . "Oh, Lord," I exclaimed. "The college must be using Grandison as a resurrection man!"

"Lower your voice," Ted said, glancing around to see if anyone heard my indiscretion. The other students appeared absorbed in their work. Ted lowered his own voice. "I think Grandison is the college resurrection man. But there's only one way to be sure."

"Oh no! You are not dragging me along on any more of your crazy adventures," I said firmly. "Last time was too much! That darned goat kicked me in the face when I shoved it up the stairs. Gave me a black eye. And *then* I had to jump out the second-story window into a tree because the dean came home early from the dinner dance. I was stuck in that blasted tree all night. I nearly froze to death. And where were you? *You* were dancing with Susan Bennett when you were supposed to be distracting the dean."

"Sorry," Ted said, not sounding sorry at all. "I got distracted by Susan. She is a real beauty! I may propose to that girl one of these days."

"You can propose to the goat for all I care," I grumbled. "Just leave me out of your stupid adventures."

Ted shrugged noncommittally as the professor strolled into the classroom to see how we were doing with the exercise. I returned my attention to the task at hand.

I suppose I shouldn't have been surprised to find myself hiding behind a large gravestone in the local cemetery around 10 p.m. a few days after this conversation took place. Ted could sell drinking water to a drowning man, so obviously I didn't stand a chance of resisting his latest crazy idea. I don't know why Ted wanted to become a doctor. He should have gone into politics.

"There," Ted said, gripping my arm and pointing. In the moonlight I saw a dark figure moving stealthily toward a freshly dug grave with a shovel over its shoulder. When the figure drew closer, I recognized the face of Grandison Harris. "See, I told you," Ted hissed in my ear.

I watched incredulously as the Gullah man dug into the grave with practiced ease. When he reached the casket, he removed a hand ax from underneath his coat and chopped into the lid of the coffin. When the hole was big enough, he removed the corpse of a middle-aged man from the grave and stuffed the body into a sack. He reburied the coffin and cleaned up the gravesite slick as you please. There was no way to tell someone had messed about with the grave. What a gruesome job, I thought with a shudder. I know it was all done to advance the progress of medicine, but I couldn't help feeling that Grandison was desecrating the dead. When folks spoke of Resurrection Day, this wasn't what they envisioned.

"Come on," Ted said, tugging at my arm.

"Come on where?" I asked. I'd seen enough for one night.

"Let's follow him," Ted said. He hurried after Grandison, crawling from tombstone to tombstone in the man's wake as the slave carried the shrouded corpse toward a donkey cart he'd parked outside the cemetery.

"Why do I do these things?" I groaned and slithered after Ted.

We followed the donkey cart through the dark streets. To my surprise, Grandison tied the cart in an alley behind the local tavern and shambled inside to buy a drink. Ted's face lit with an evil grin as the Gullah disappeared into the bar. "I've got a great idea," Ted said to me.

"Oh no!" I said, remembering the goat.

"Oh yes," said Ted. We held a quick conference. Well, truth be told, Ted told me his brilliant plan, and I tried to talk him out of it. I was still protesting as Ted pulled the corpse out of the donkey cart and carried it into the bushes, leaving me to crawl into the empty sack, trying hard not to remember who had just occupied this space.

I'd just finished hiding myself in the sack when Grandison staggered out of the bar. He untied the donkey and climbed unsteadily into the seat, muttering curses under his breath.

As the cart moved down the alley, I peered out of the sack at the resurrection man and called, "Grandison! Grandison, I'm cold. Buy me a drink!"

RESURRECTION MAN

Grandison jumped straight up in the air. I've never in my life seen anyone move so fast. Dropping the reins, he leapt over the side of the cart in a single bound, shouting, "Get yer own durn drink 'cause I am outta here!"

Grandison was out of sight by the time I disentangled myself from the blasted sack. I could hear Ted laughing, and when I stood up in the back of the cart, I saw him rolling about on the road, clutching his stomach and raising a huge cloud of dust. I rubbed a hand over my mouth, trying to hide my smile. Okay, so this crazy adventure wasn't nearly as bad as the goat.

I jumped down from the cart and hurried over to Ted. "So what do we do with the cadaver?" I asked. Wiping tears of laughter from his eyes, Ted staggered to his feet.

"We put it back into the cart and park it in front of Grandison's place," Ted said.

So that's what we did.

The resurrection man continued his gruesome task long after I finished my medical training. I heard later that he stuck to his work after the Civil War, when he could have walked away as a free man. Overall, I can't say that I approved of grave robbing, even for the cause of science. But I must admit that between the two of them, Ted and Grandison provided me with the happiest memory I have from my college days.

22

The Operation

I was in law school when the South withdrew from the Union. I had a duty to serve my family and my state, so I left the university to join the Confederate Army. I served from the beginning of the war until the bitter end, when Lee surrendered his Army of Northern Virginia on April 9, 1865.

War is terrible. The scars—both physical and mental—that I bear from that period have changed me irrevocably. Many of my friends died on the battlefield; still more died in the makeshift hospitals. I hated those hospitals. They were hastily improvised and entirely inadequate to the need. The sanitary conditions were appalling.

Out of the 115 surgeons serving in the US Surgeon General's office at the outbreak of the war, only twenty-four resigned to form the nucleus of the Confederate medical services. As if that weren't bad enough, the nursing was completely primitive. Both sides relied heavily on untrained male nurses. It gave me shivers to think of it. I counted myself lucky that the few wounds I received did not require hospitalization.

Hospitalization, to my mind, was the equivalent of a death sentence. I held this truth indisputable after the Battle of

Fredericksburg. My brother and I were assigned to different units, and we became separated during the battle. When a close friend told me he'd seen my brother shot down during the battle, I scoured the fields for days, searching for his body. Then someone told me they'd seen my brother in the hospital. Filled with hope, I hurried to the hospital as fast as my legs would carry me. The entrance was partially blocked by a stack of bloody severed limbs crawling with flies. It turned my stomach. Hurrying past, I made my way to my brother's bedside, only to discover that my brother's left leg was in the pile outside.

My brother was in a bad way when I arrived. The man in the next cot told me his wounded leg was septic and was cut off without the aid of anesthesia. My brother was delirious with fever and shock of the amputation. He did not recognize me. I sat beside the cot holding his hand, trying not to breathe through my nose, for the smell of infection, sweat-soaked bodies, and urine was unbearable. He died less than an hour after I arrived.

After the war I learned that mortality from disease and wounds was far higher than from bullets. Remembering those hospitals, I believed it.

I resumed my legal studies after the war and graduated with honors. I threw myself into my work, starting my own law firm and building a good reputation among my fellow attorneys. I worked long hours into the night, determined to succeed. My family urged me to slow down. They wanted me to marry and have a family, but I was content to be a bachelor; too absorbed in my work to give love a second thought.

Nearly a decade passed in this manner. Then I attended a political dinner party at my new partner's request and met

THE OPERATION

Madeleine. I fell like a rock. She was a blond beauty with more than her fair share of brains and wit. And she had the most gorgeous hazel eyes I'd ever seen. Madeleine lived far away in south Georgia, too far for me to visit every week. But she lived near the railroad, so I traveled back and forth to Georgia once a month, stopping overnight at a hotel in Marietta on my way there and back again.

After courting Madeleine for six months, I wrote to her parents asking for her hand in marriage. Upon receiving their consent, I purchased a ring and planned a surprise trip to south Georgia, where I intended to propose to Madeleine in person. I spent the first leg of my journey south planning every detail of my proposal. I barely glanced at my hotel room as I tossed my bags onto the bed and hurried down the stairs for dinner. I was picturing Madeleine's face when I would show her the diamond ring currently burning a hole in my waistcoat pocket. She would be so surprised! I chuckled aloud as I took my seat in the restaurant and ordered a glass of wine to celebrate the occasion.

I limited myself to one glass, for I had a long journey on the morrow and wanted to look my best when I arrived at my darling girl's home in the afternoon. My world looked very rosy as I headed upstairs to my room, intending to retire early.

As I stepped into the third-floor hallway, I was overwhelmed by a tide of odors, the like of which I had not smelled since my war days. The hall stank of blood, sweat, urine, and ether. I gasped, and my hand flew up to cover my nose as I peered around in astonishment. What could be causing such a smell?

To my horror I realized the hallway was gone, replaced by a long room filled with cot upon cot of injured soldiers.

Bandages were caked with blood, limbs were swollen with infection, men were groaning in pain. Directly in front of me, two men bent solemnly over a wounded soldier on a pallet. The man at the head of the pallet held a cone over the patient's face, obviously administering anesthesia to the soldier. The other man—a surgeon—stood beside the soldier's left leg. A tourniquet was tied at the thigh. The skin had been cut open several inches below the tourniquet, and the muscles were pulled up to expose the bone. The surgeon held an amputation saw in his hand, and I heard the rough sawing noise it made as he cut through the man's thighbone.

I yelped in terror, reminded of my poor, tormented brother. Whirling in a panic, I raced down to the lobby and knocked down the bellman who was entering the door as I exited.

"Sir, what's wrong?" the lad asked as I apologized and helped him up. I brushed a shaking hand across my forehead and blurted out my story. The boy wouldn't believe me, of course. I hardly believed it myself. But the boy nodded. "This building was used as a hospital during the war," he explained. "You aren't the first to see ghosts from the war."

He spoke in such a matter-of-fact tone that I felt ashamed of my reaction. But there was no way I was going back upstairs. I had nothing against the hotel per se, but I refused to share my floor with ghosts. I tipped the bellman a dollar and asked him to fetch my luggage. I informed the management that I was leaving early and carried my belongings outside. It was late and I was tired, so I marched over to the railroad depot and spent the night on a very hard bench. It was not comfortable.

I caught the first train out of Marietta and left without a backward glance. That was the last time, I decided, that I would patronize that particular hotel. I had my own mental ghosts to deal with from those terrible war days. I had no desire to deal with real ghosts as well.

I fingered the ring in my pocket and turned my thoughts back to Madeleine and the future.

23

The Devil Is Going to Get You

WASHINGTON

Abram was a fortunate man. He ran the local tavern, so he had plenty of money in his pocket. When he built a racetrack near the tavern, he grew wealthier still. He married a beautiful lady, and he was as dewy eyed over his bride twenty years later as he'd been when he was a blushing groom. To top off his blessings, Abram had purchased a fine racehorse named Babylon that could run like the wind. Abram was so proud of that horse that he treated Babylon like family, to the chagrin of his lovely wife, Nancy.

"You'd have that horse eating at the dinner table if I'd let you," she scolded Abram, giving him a kiss on the top of his head to let him know she wasn't really angry.

Things started to go wrong for Abram the Sunday his wife invited the dad-blamed revival preacher to dinner. Abram would sometimes accompany his wife to church just to please her, but he was born to a different religion and he would not abandon his faith, even for Nancy. So Abram told the preacher man when the minister tried to convert him over the roast beef.

"Give it up, preacher. Your ways aren't mine," Abram said, waving his fork in the general direction of the minister.

"You'd better mend your ways, Abram Simon, or the devil's going to get you one of these days," the minister exclaimed, his cheeks going red with passion as he cut fiercely into the beef. "Those men who frequent that tavern of yours are drunk more than they are sober. *And* I hear there's betting on those horses that you run on your racetrack. It's the work of Satan, I tell you. You're trying to outrun the devil, and it won't work, not even on a horse as fast as Babylon." The minister was sawing so hard at his meat that Abram reckoned he was going to put a hole in the plate. "Babylon! What a name for an animal. Babylon fell, you know, and so will you!"

The minister preached hellfire and damnation at Abram all during dinner, while Nancy nodded her head soberly and said the occasional "amen." Abram glared at his beloved helpmeet down the length of the table, suspecting her of egging the minister on. She hated the masculine wallpaper he'd ordered for the ballroom, and this invitation to the revival preacher was her way of getting revenge.

Abram affected indifference to the minister's words, but the next evening when he was exercising Babylon, he glanced casually around the racetrack and saw a sinister man in black sitting on the woodpile. The man was wearing a fancy top hat, and the angular eyes in his sharp face glowed red. Abram did not need the pointed goatee and the slightly fanged smile to know who this was. The woodpile started to char and smoke around the dark figure.

Abram gave a shout of dismay, and Babylon leapt forward at a gallop, swerving off the racetrack and heading for home at top speed. When Abram glanced back, the woodpile was empty. The logs in the top layer were burnt black just where the devil had perched.

THE DEVIL IS GOING TO GET YOU

Abram was sweating profusely when he reached the stable yard and swung off his shaking horse. How strange he should be sweating, Abram thought in the detached manner that denotes extreme shock, when his whole body felt ice cold.

Abram walked Babylon around and around the paddock until he was cool enough to put in the stable. By the time Babylon was settled for the night, Abram's heartbeat had settled too. But he couldn't stop thinking about the devil. The minister had said the devil was going to get him, and the very next day Satan had appeared at Abram's racetrack. It was uncanny.

Abram hurried inside on trembling legs. Should he tell Nancy what he'd seen? No, of course not! No one in her right mind would believe he'd seen the devil on the racetrack. Abram barely believed it himself.

After downing a couple of shots of whisky, Abram decided it had been a trick of the light. It was dusk after all, and the shadows had been thick under the tall trees. He hadn't *really* seen the devil. Abram relaxed and went into the parlor to greet his wife.

Two weeks later Abram was cleaning glasses behind the bar when his eye was drawn to a small round table in the corner of the room. He frowned. Where had that table come from? The hat stand was traditionally placed in that corner. Suddenly a man in black appeared in one of the chairs. A fancy top hat materialized on the table beside him. The sinister figure gave Abram a knowing, fanged smile, dark eyes glowing red above his sharp beard. Abram glimpsed a bit of tail hanging from the back of the chair and let out a yelp of terror. Instantly, devil, top hat, and table vanished in a puff of smoke, revealing the old hat stand in its accustomed place.

"Are you all right Abram?" asked the butcher, one of Abram's customers, suspiciously, glancing from the tavern owner to the hat stand and back.

"Fine, fine," Abram said, his voice several pitches higher than normal. The customers were casting curious glances his way, so he turned his attention back to the glass he was polishing. It shook noticeably in his hand. This would never do. Abram put the glass down with a thump. It rattled uncertainly and almost toppled over. The butcher stared at the drinking glass and then raised an eyebrow at Abram. Abram grinned sheepishly and hastened into the back room.

"What am I going to do?" he groaned, clutching his head in his hands. He took a deep breath and then straightened his spine. He was going to go down fighting, that's what he was going to do. Maybe he couldn't outrace the devil, but he was going to try!

Over the next few years, Abram grew used to the occasional sighting of the man in the top hat. In fact, it won him several races. Babylon, the only other creature in the world who could see the devil as well as Abram, grew wings whenever the devil showed up by the racetrack. Unfortunately the racetrack wasn't the only place the devil turned up. Abram sometimes heard hoofbeats on the road behind him when he rode Babylon home at night. He could see the devil trotting about a hundred yards back on a coal-black stallion with flaming eyes, but only if he looked from the corners of his eyes. If he turned his head, the road behind him was empty. Whenever Babylon heard the devil's hoofbeats, he flew down the road at top speed, but he could never shake the pursuer.

Once Abram tried to shoot the devil. He turned sideways in the saddle and fired three times into the empty air behind him. The bullets exploded in midair, sending clouds of acrid smoke billowing into the sky. The smoke smelled of fire and brimstone. Abram gave a shout of fear and spurred Babylon away at speed. Faster and faster the great horse ran. But the devil was not far behind.

Abram never told anyone about his visions. Who would believe him? Folks thought he'd gone a bit strange in the head. A nervous condition, they called it. And they shook their heads incredulously when he had his gravesite built on top of a knoll instead of in the family cemetery. "I need an unobstructed view," he told his wife, Nancy. "I need to be able to see all around in case the devil comes for me when I pass."

Abram built a thick stone wall around the gravesite and gave orders that his wife should bury him standing up with a musket at his side.

"Why ever do you want to do that?" Nancy asked, puzzled.

"So I can shoot the devil when he comes for me," said Abram firmly.

Nancy could not talk him out of the notion.

In 1824 Abram fell gravely ill. He knew he was dying and reminded Nancy of her promise. She wept as she kissed him and assured Abram that his instructions would be followed to the letter. Behind his wife's beloved face, Abram thought he glimpsed a dark figure in a top hat. Then the world faded away, and Abram was gone.

Abram had no idea how much time had passed when he suddenly found himself astride Babylon with a musket by his side. Horse and rider stood beside a low stone wall on top of a moonlit knoll. Abram glanced blankly at the gravestone behind the wall. There was something familiar about it, something significant. But it wasn't important right now. Right now he had to ride. Abram called to his horse, and Babylon reared and turned in one smooth motion. Then they were on the road, galloping flat out. Abram urged his horse into greater speed, his heart thundering within him. The enemy was approaching. He knew it in his bones. Abram looked back and saw a man with a sharp face and red eyes following him on a black steed. "Faster," Abram urged his horse. "Faster. The devil is going to get you!" Behind him, the devil laughed.

24

On the Tracks

LAWRENCEVILLE

It was a menacing black night—the kind that swallows light and makes grown men hide under the covers until dawn. Danger lurked in every shadow, and I hesitated a moment before I opened the door to the cloakroom. For some reason I pictured Death looming behind that massive portal, waiting—scythe poised—to mow me down.

My body trembled with nerves as I skittered out to the train and climbed into the engine. The depot's gas lanterns did nothing to expel the gloom. In a strange reversal of the natural order, they actually made the shadows deeper. Strange shapes seemed to flicker at the corners of my eyes, and I jumped when the fireman climbed into the engine. He gave me an odd stare before stoking the firebox and attending the boiler.

I was working as an engineer on the new narrow-gauge railroad running between Lawrenceville and Suwanee. We began service in December of 1881 and brought loads of cut timber down from the lumber camps to the bustle metropolis of Atlanta. It was a good job—most nights. But tonight was different; don't ask me how. My nerves were taut all day; making me so cross my wife sent me out to the barn to work off my temper. The thought of tonight's ride scared the dickens out of me, which was silly. Most nights the run was mind-bogglingly dull.

I couldn't help thinking of train accidents. You heard stories of engineers who had premonitions just before their last run. But I hadn't dreamed of train wrecks or seen any visions. I just felt . . . nervous. As if some evil pressure were pushing against my mind, against my body, trying to get in, for what foul purpose I could not imagine.

I said none of this to my fireman. I just started the locomotive rolling down the track, straining my eyes to see in the gloom. The night seemed to eat the lights only a few yards in front of the engine. There were no stars, and no moon shown through the thick dark clouds that hung like vultures in the night sky. The wind howled through the tortured trees like a pack of giant wolves.

I shuddered and opened the throttle. I wanted to get this run over as fast as possible. Occasionally a gust would buffet the train, shaking it from front to back. Perhaps this terrible wind was the cause of my foreboding. Perhaps the wind would blow the train off the track! Tornados were not impossible this time of year.

I drove automatically, my jittery eyes swerving this way and that, from track to murky meadow, from track to writhing woodland, from track to brooding crossroad. Cold chills ran up and down my spine. I kept expecting a black funnel to stretch its finger down from the darkness overhead and snatch me up, train and all.

There is only so long the body can stay on high alert before the tension takes its toll. By the time the train entered Adair Woods, I was exhausted. My shoulders slumped, and I laughed suddenly in relief. I must be mad. There was no tornado. No menace lurking. This was ridiculous.

Then I saw a figure leap onto the tracks in front of me. A huge figure, taller than a man—taller than a horse. It cavorted in the light from the headlamps, leaping back and forth across the tracks like a ballet dancer. I gasped, reaching for the brake. What was *that?*

Suddenly the figure leapt into the center of the tracks, massive hairy arms thrust on equally massive hips, its face—half human, half ape—glared menacingly at me in the light of the headlamps. It bent forward slightly as if the train bearing down on it was a beast to be wrestled into submission. I shouted in alarm and hit the brake, staring into huge red eyes that glowed like coals of brimstone from a hundred yards away, then fifty, then ten as the train shuddered and coughed and screeched its way to a halt.

The moment the train stopped, the creature vanished. I gasped, completely nonplussed. The fireman gave a shout of frustration, wanting to know why I'd stopped the train. His face wrinkled suddenly. "Ew. What's that smell?" The scent of garbage, decay, and raw meat filled the cab. Suddenly the whole engine shook as a huge body thumped against the locomotive. My body went rigid with shock and then filled with tingling energy from head to toe.

"What in God's name is that?" roared the fireman as the engine shook under a second blow. Through the front window I saw the creature climbing up the front of the engine. It had to be nine feet tall and nearly as broad. Those burning eyes belonged in hell. For some reason it wanted to get into my engine. No, what it wanted was me. Me and my fireman. It wanted to kill us.

I stared at the creature, mesmerized by the hatred twisting its half-human face. What had we done to make it despise us so?

ON THE TRACKS

Had a train killed its mate? Had humans forced it from its home territory?

"Get us out of here!" The fireman screamed in my ear, shaking me desperately to snap me out of my hypnotized state. "Do you want to die?"

I did *not* want to die. I released the brake, counting the too-slow seconds until the brake vacuum reached twenty-one. Then I opened the throttle just as the huge man-beast slammed his fists onto the front window. I recoiled and the fireman cursed.

"Hurry! Hurry!" he shouted as the creature rained blows onto each of the windows in turn. Slowly, far too slowly, the engine gained speed.

"More power!" I howled. The fireman leapt to the boiler to do what he could. Tiny cracks appeared in the windows like threads in a spider web. Any moment now one of them would shatter and the creature could enter the cab!

Then the wind I had feared so much just an hour ago came to our aid. A huge gust slammed against the locomotive, shaking it so hard that the beast lost its grip and fell off. It was on its feet in seconds, pounding after us. I could see the glow of its eyes through the side window as it came up beside the cab, stretching a massive hairy arm toward the handrail so that it could begin another assault.

"My kingdom for a rifle," shouted the fireman, glaring at the beast.

"Go, go, go!" I urged the engine on. The train howled as it leapt forward, gaining moment now. It sounded as menacing as the wind had an hour ago. The train was my weapon, and if the creature were foolish enough to get in my way, I would mow it down. For one long moment it raced defiantly beside us, glaring

175

death from its red eyes. Then it roared in defeat and vanished into the woods.

Seconds later the train swept out of Adair Woods into open pastureland with farms on either side of the tracks. Thank God for those farms. Farms meant people with rifles and dogs that would not look with favor on an unwarranted attack by a monster. I sagged with relief but kept the train at full throttle for the rest of our journey. It wasn't until I saw the lights of the Suwanee depot ahead of me that I slowed the train. The run was nearly over.

The fireman said gruffly: "Are you going to tell them about that . . . that . . . *creature* that attacked the train."

"I'll have to," I replied. "How else can we explain the damage to the glass? But I bet you a dime they won't believe me."

I was wrong. They did believe me, and my fireman collected on the dime bet. Apparently the strange man-ape had been spotted several times in the vicinity of Lawrenceville, frightening more than one family. It had been driven off by a posse of men with rifles and must have taken up residence in the Adair Woods shortly thereafter.

For a few weeks after our encounter, parties of hunters scoured the woods, stalking the man-ape. No one ever caught it.

I kept my rifle on hand during my nightly runs for the next six months, but the creature never returned. Thank God.

25

Silver

January 25, 1894

My dear brother,

Maude and I were thrilled to receive your letter of the 20th and have read it to the entire family. Brother, we miss you sorely and hope you are well, living as you do in the "Wild West." Our eldest boy sketched some romanticized pictures of you in a ten-gallon hat with two six-shooters at your side. He thinks of you as another Wild Bill Hickok! I haven't the heart to tell him you own a small farm in Oregon and shoot groundhogs with a rifle. Enclosed is one of the sketches. I hope it will give you and Leticia a hearty laugh.

You asked in your letter why I do not use the ford across the Satilla River, choosing instead the longer journey over the covered bridge. Brother, there is some foundation to my odd behavior. It is a strange story I have to tell, and one that I fear you will not believe. But I swear by all I hold dear that it is true.

Last December I was called out to a difficult birthing. Mrs. Gammage—you will remember her as Miss Olivia

Hardy—was brought to bed with twin girls. I attended her as physician and longtime friend of the family. It was a difficult birth. One twin was breech and the other had the cord tangled around her tiny neck. But all ended well, and I left mother and daughters sleeping quietly, departing the farm around 2 a.m.

I was riding my new saddle horse—a lovely roan mare named Star of Dawn. The night was cool, and clouds covered the sky. As I journeyed across the dark countryside, a light rain began to fall. I hunched my shoulders against the cold rain, pulled the brim of my hat down over my eyes, and endured.

On such dark nights I am grateful that my horse knows the road, for I gave her little direction. I was half asleep in the saddle by the time we reached the ford at Sattila River. Star of Dawn waded into the river, and a splash of cold water snapped me awake. We were halfway across the river when a blast of hot air smashed down upon us, parting the water down to the gravel bottom and causing the trees on either bank to thrash wildly. My hat went flying into the river as silver light illuminated the heavens above. I shielded my eyes, which pained me. Such an introduction of brilliant light was startling after so much darkness.

Star of Dawn reared, screaming in panic, and I had a hard time staying in the saddle. The wind grew less forceful, and the river rushed back, forcing the mare to drop on all fours to maintain her balance. I hung on for dear life, tears streaming from my light-stricken eyes.

Slowly my gaze adjusted to the massive light pouring down from above. It turned the waters of the river to

Silver

glittering silver with no shadows. I stared upward at a giant round object hovering just above the treetops. The silver light sprang from a ring around the bottom of the flattish sphere. Its silver light illuminated the underside of the dark clouds, still spitting rain upon the flying monstrosity.

Chills raced through my body at the sight. My legs closed automatically around Star of Dawn, urging her forward. In this moment of utter terror and disorientation, I wanted to get out away from the ford as quickly as possible.

Tearing my eyes from the hovering saucer, I looked ahead and then hauled frantically on the reins, every muscle in my body tensed in shock. Four bright figures were walking along the bank, hulking forms in puffy reflective clothing that dazzled the eye. The creatures had round metallic heads and horrible reflective flat plates where their faces should be. With two arms and two legs apiece, they might almost have been human, save for those terrible, distorted heads. My stomach heaved in horror.

Then, in a flash of memory, I remembered a sketch from a Jules Verne story showing a man wearing an underwater suit. The figures standing on the riverbank looked a bit like the man in the sketch. I peered at the figures again, suddenly intrigued. The horror of the moment suddenly abated under my scientific curiosity. My horse did not feel the same. Star of Dawn, terrified beyond reason, reared with a bone-chilling scream I was unprepared for my horse's panicked movement and slid from the saddle, smashing into the river at high speed and bruising my head and shoulders as they cannoned into the gravel river bottom. The heavy jolt shocked every nerve in my body. I breathed water, choked, and leapt to my feet in one

179

terrified motion. Star of Dawn had already reached the far bank when I surfaced from my impromptu bath.

I whirled to face the shining figures looming above me on the bank. I had lost my means of escape, and my heart pounded against my ribs as I wondered what to do. Were the creatures hostile? Would they kill me? Should I follow my horse? I didn't want to turn my back on them.

The hot wind pouring from the bottom of the glowing sphere was already drying my dripping hair as I stood indecisively in the flowing river. The figures on the bank paid me no heed. They raised their strange metallic heads . . . masks . . . whatever and gestured upward toward the hovering sphere brightening the rain clouds.

Suddenly, between one blink of my dazzled eyes and the next, the figures were gone. My pulse gave a painful throb and I shouted in disbelief. I gazed upward at the round silver shape hovering in the sky, expecting to see . . . I know not what.

The heavy wind came again, pushing the river water out of its bank and knocking me over. The glowing silver sphere accelerated suddenly, traveling up and up into the sky, piercing through the heavy rain clouds. For a moment I saw a silvery lining inside the translucent clouds, still moving upward. Then it was gone.

Freed from the force of the hot wind, the river hurled itself back into its bank. I clutched at a large rock to keep myself from being swept away as water poured over me. The muscles of my arms corded with the strain, but I managed to hang on until the water calmed and resumed its normal path. I surfaced, hauling air into my lungs in a great gasping breath, and my feet stumbled in the loose gravel, seeking purchase. I found stabile footing at last and stood panting in fear and disbelief, the river water tugging at my waistcoat as it rolled past. I turned around and around, staring dazedly from bank to bank in the sudden, blinding darkness. Had I just seen what I thought I had seen?

After many minutes I realized I was standing in the middle of the river in the rain with no horse and no way to get home save my two trembling legs. I staggered through the water to the far bank and hauled myself out. I could use some of that silver light right about now, I thought with grim amusement. What a pickle I was in!

When I reached the top of the bank, my foot accidently kicked a small object lying on the ground. It glimmered silver in the rain-swept darkness, picking up light from I know not what source. Clumsily I picked it up. It was a rectangular object, about half an inch thick and eight inches long. One side was inlaid with some kind of nonreflective glass. I stared at the strange box in fascination. It must have been dropped from one of the silvery figures that had vanished so spectacularly before my astonished eyes.

I heard a neigh from the opposite bank and whirled, trembling in renewed anxiety. I saw the dark outline of a horse standing beside the ford. It was Star of Dawn. Oh what a good horse! She had come back to find me. I called and she gave an answering whicker and waded into the river. A moment later we were reunited, and she carried me the rest of the way home in safety.

And that, my brother, was the very last time I ever used the ford on Satilla River. If any strange objects appear in the

SILVER

sky, they will have a hard time blowing me away underneath the roof of the covered bridge!

This letter grows long and Maude calls me to dinner, so I will close now and write again later. I am enclosing a second sketch made by my eldest son. It depicts the strange object I saw in the sky. You will notice how humorously he has drawn the wide-eyed man in the river. I told him not to be cheeky, and he assured me that he would not have fallen into the water if he had been the one observing the silver sky sphere. Whatever shall I do with such a cheeky lad?

Maude and the children send their love to you and Leticia.

Your fond elder brother,
Harry

Resources

Akamatsu, Rhetta. *Haunted Marietta*. Charleston, SC: Haunted America, 2009.

Alan, Ian. *Georgia Ghosts: They Are Among Us*. Birmingham, AL: Sweetwater Press Produced by Cliff Road Books, 2005.

Asfar, Daniel, and Edrick Thay. *Ghost Stories of America*. Edmonton, AB: Ghost House Books, 2001.

Bailey, Cornelia Walker, with Christena Bledsoe. *God, Dr. Buzzard, and the Bolito Man*. New York: Anchor Books, 2000.

Barber, Christina A. *Spirits of Georgia's Southern Crescent*. Atglen, PA: Schiffer Publishing, Ltd., 2008.

Battle, Kemp P. *Great American Folklore*. New York: Doubleday & Company, Inc., 1986.

Bender, William N. *Haunted Atlanta and Beyond*. Athens, GA: Hill Street Press, 2005.

Botkin, B. A., ed. *A Treasury of American Folklore*. New York: Crown, 1944.

Boyle, Virginia Frazer. *Devil Tales: Black Americana Folk-Lore*. New York: Harper & Brothers Publishers, 1900.

Brown, Alan. *Haunted Georgia*. Mechanicsburg, PA: Stackpole Books, 2008.

———. *Stories from the Haunted South*. Jackson: University Press of Mississippi, 2004.

Brunvand, Jan Harold. *The Choking Doberman and Other Urban Legends.* New York: W. W. Norton, 1984.

———. *The Vanishing Hitchhiker.* New York: W. W. Norton, 1981.

Buxton, Geordie, and Ed Macy. *Haunted Harbor.* Charleston, SC: Haunted America, 2005.

Buxton, Geordie. *Haunted Plantations.* Charleston, SC: Arcadia Publishing, 2007.

Byrd, Georgia R. *Haunted Savannah.* Guilford, CT: Globe Pequot Press, 2011.

Caskey, James. *Haunted Savannah.* Savannah, GA: Bonaventture Books, 2005.

Christchurchfredericka.org. "Walking through History into the Future with Christ." Accessed 2/14/2012 at www.christchurchfrederica.org/721806.

Christian, Reese. *Ghosts of Atlanta.* Charleston, SC: Haunted America, 2008.

Cobb, Al. *Savannah's Ghosts.* Atglen, PA: Schiffer Publishing Ltd., 2010.

Coffin, Tristram. P., and Hennig Cohen, eds. *Folklore in America.* New York: Doubleday & AMP, 1966.

———. *Folklore from the Working Folk of America.* New York: Doubleday, 1973.

Cohen, Daniel, and Susan Cohen. *Hauntings & Horrors.* New York: Dutton Children's Books, 2002.

Cox, Dale. "The Ghost of the St. Simons Lighthouse." Exploresouthernhistory.com. Accessed 2/14/2012 at www.exploresouthernhistory.com/gastsimons2.

DeBolt, Margaret Wayt. *Savannah Spectres and Other Strange Tales.* Virginia Beach, VA: The Donning Company/ Publishers, 1984.

Dolgner, Beth. *Georgia Spirits and Specters.* Atglen, PA: Schiffer Publishing Ltd., 2009.

Dorson, R. M. *America in Legend.* New York: Pantheon Books, 1973.

Downer, Deborah L. *Classic American Ghost Stories.* Little Rock, AR: August House Publishers, Inc.

Duffey, Barbara. *Banshees, Bugles and Belles: True Ghost Stories of Georgia.* Berryville, VA: Rockbridge Publishing Company, 1995.

Easley, Nicole Carlson. *Savannah Folklore.* Atglen, PA: Schiffer Publishing Ltd., 2010.

Editors of *Life* magazine. *The Life Treasury of American Folklore.* New York: Time Inc., 1961.

Erdoes, Richard, and Alfonso Ortiz. *American Indian Myths and Legends.* New York: Pantheon Books, 1984.

Farrant, Don. *Ghosts of the Georgia Coast.* Sarasota, FL: Pineapple Press, Inc., 2002.

Fisher, Jeffrey. *Haunted Georgia: The Haunted Hotels, Inns and Bed and Breakfasts of GA.* Seattle, WA: Amazon Digital Services.

Flanagan, J. T., and A. P. Hudson. *The American Folk Reader.* New York: A. S. Barnes & Co., 1958.

Georgia Writers' Project. *Drums and Shadows.* Los Angeles: Indo-European Publishing, 2010.

Gibbons, Faye. *Hook Moon Night.* New York: Morrow Junior Books, 1997.

Graydon, Nell S. *Tales of Edisto.* Orangeburg, SC: Sandlapper Publishing Co., Inc., 1955.

Green, R. Edwin, and Mary A. *St. Simons: A Summary of Its History.* Glynncounty.com. Accessed 2/14/2012 at www.glynncounty.com/History_and_Lore/Ed_Green.

Hartsfield, Mariella Glenn. *Tall Betsy and Dunce Baby: South Georgia Folktales.* Athens: University of Georgia Press, 1987.

Hauck, Dennis William. *Haunted Places: The National Directory.* New York: Penguin Books, 1994.

Higginson, Thomas Wentworth. "Negro Spirituals." Boston: *Atlantic Monthly,* June 1867. Accessed 3/4/2012 at http://xroads.virginia.edu/~hyper/twh/higg.html.

Holub, Joan. *The Haunted States of America.* New York: Aladdin Paperbacks, 2001.

Jekyllclub.com. "Ghosts of Jekyll Island's Past." Accessed on 2/23/2012 at www.jekyllclub.com/2010/10/26/the-ghosts-of-jekyll-islands-past-4.

Jekyll-island-family-adventures.com. "Strange Mysteries of Famous Ghosts and Haunted Places at Jekyll Island's Historic District." Accessed 2/23/2012 at www.jekyll-island-family-adventures.com/strange-mysteries.html.

Johnson, Scott A. *The Mayor's Guide: The Stately Ghosts of Augusta*. Augusta, GA: Harbor House, 2005.

Killion, Ronald G., and Charles T. Waller. *A Treasury of Georgia Folklore*. Marietta, GA: Cherokee Publishing Company, 1972.

Leach, M. *The Rainbow Book of American Folk Tales and Legends*. New York: The World Publishing Co., 1958.

Leeming, David, and Jake Pagey. *Myths, Legends & Folktales of America*. New York: Oxford University Press, 1999.

Miles, Jim. *Weird Georgia*. Nashville, TN: Cumberland House Publishing, Inc., 2000.

Miles, Jim, Mark Sceurman, and Mark Moran. *Weird Georgia*. New York: Sterling Publishing Co., Inc., 2006.

Mitchell, Faith. *Hoodoo Medicine*. Columbia, SC: Summerhouse Press, 1999.

Mott, A. S. *Ghost Stories of America*, Vol. II. Edmonton, AB: Ghost House Books, 2003.

Nmhm.washingtondc.museum. "The Smell of Ether, the Odor of Blood." Washington, DC: National Museum of Health & Medicine. Accessed on 9/29/2012 at http://nmhm.washingtondc.museum/exhibits/nationswounds/surgery.html.

Norman, Michael, and Beth Scott. *Historic Haunted America*. New York: Tor Books, 1995.

Peck, Catherine, ed. *A Treasury of North American Folk Tales*. New York: W. W. Norton, 1998.

Pinckney, Roger. *Blue Roots.* Orangeburg, SC: Sandlapper
Publishing Co., Inc., 2003.

Polley, J., ed. *American Folklore and Legend.* New York:
Reader's Digest Association, 1978.

Reevy, Tony. *Ghost Train!* Lynchburg, VA: TLC Publishing,
1998.

Rhodes, Don. *Mysteries and Legends of Georgia.* Guilford, CT:
Globe Pequot Press, 2010.

Roberts, Nancy. *Georgia Ghosts.* Winston-Salem, NC: John F.
Blair, Publisher, 1997.

———. *Ghosts from the Coast.* Chapel Hill: University of
North Carolina Press, 2001.

———. *The Haunted South.* Columbia: University of South
Carolina Press, 1988.

Rule, Leslie. *Coast to Coast Ghosts.* Kansas City, KS: Andrews
McMeel Publishing, 2001.

Schwartz, Alvin. *Scary Stories to Tell in the Dark.* New York:
Harper Collins, 1981.

Skinner, Charles M. *American Myths and Legends,* Vol. 1.
Philadelphia: J. B. Lippincott, 1903.

———. *Myths and Legends of Our Own Land,* Vol. 1 & 2.
Philadelphia: J. B. Lippincott, 1896.

Smith, Gordon Burns, and, Anna Habersham Wright
Smith. *Ghost Dances and Shadow Pantomimes,* Vol. 1.
Milledgeville, GA: Boyd Publishing, 2004.

Spence, Lewis. *North American Indians: Myths and Legends
Series.* London: Bracken Books, 1985.

Students of Haskell Institute. *Myths, Legends, Superstitions of North American Indian Tribes.* Cherokee, NC: Cherokee Publications, 1995.

Thay, Edrick. *Ghost Stories of the Old South.* Edmonton, AB: Ghost House Books, 2003.

Underwood, Corinna. *Haunted History of Atlanta and North Georgia.* Atglen, PA: Schiffer Publishing, Ltd., 2008.

Wangler, Chris. *Ghost Stories of Georgia.* Auburn, WA: Lone Pine Publishing International, Inc., 2006.

Wells, Jeffery. *Bigfoot in Georgia.* Enumclaw, WA: Pine Winds Press, 2010.

Windham, Kathryn Tucker. *13 Georgia Ghosts and Jeffery.* Tuscaloosa: University of Alabama Press, 1973.

Zeitlin, Steven J., Amy J. Kotkin, and Holly Cutting Baker. *A Celebration of American Family Folklore.* New York: Pantheon Books, 1982.

Zepke, Terrance. *Lowcountry Voodoo.* Sarasota, FL: Pineapple Press, Inc., 2009.

About the Author

Author S. E. Schlosser has been telling stories since she was a child, when games of "let's pretend" quickly built themselves into full-length stories. A graduate of the Institute of Children's Literature and Rutgers University, she also created and maintains www.AmericanFolklore.net, where she shares a wealth of stories from all fifty states, some dating back to the origins of America.

About the Illustrator

Artist Paul Hoffman trained in painting and printmaking. His first extensive illustration work on assignment was in Egypt, drawing ancient wall reliefs for the University of Chicago. His work graces books of many genres—including children's titles, textbooks, short story collections, natural history volumes, and numerous cookbooks. For *Spooky Georgia* he employed a scratchboard technique and an active imagination.